Assessing Learning

Librarians and Teachers as Partners

VIOLET H. HARADA
JOAN M. YOSHINA

LIBRARIES
UNLIMITED
A Member of the Greenwood Publishing Group

Westport, Connecticut · London

British Library Cataloguing in Publication Data is available.

Copyright © 2005 by Libraries Unlimited

All rights reserved. No portion of this book may be reproduced, by any process or technique, without the express written consent of the publisher.

Library of Congress Control Number: 2005927742
ISBN: 1–59158–200–8

First published in 2005

Libraries Unlimited, 88 Post Road West, Westport, CT 06881
A Member of the Greenwood Publishing Group, Inc.
www.lu.com

Printed in the United States of America

The paper used in this book complies with the Permanent Paper Standard issued by the National Information Standards Organization (Z39.48–1984).

10 9 8 7 6 5 4 3 2

Contents

Illustrations   *xi*

Acknowledgments   *xv*

Introduction   *xvi*

Chapter 1   Assessment in Today's School   1
    What Is Assessment?   1
    What's Happening with Assessment in Our Schools?   1
       Students Must Be Central Partners in Assessment   2
       Teachers Must View Assessment as Integral
          and Ongoing   3
    How Does *No Child Left Behind* Impact Assessment?   3
    Do Effective Library Media Programs
       Make a Difference?   4
    What Is the Library Media Specialist's Role?   5
       Benefits of Assessment   5
       Essential Questions for the Library Media Specialist   6
    Conclusion   7
    References   7

Chapter 2   Assessment in the Library Media Center   10
    What Do We Assess?   10
       Authentic Learning   10
       Information Literacy   11
       Relationship to Content Standards   13
    How Do We Assess for Learning?   13
    What Are the Necessary First Steps?   14
    Conclusion   16
    References   17

Chapter 3   Tools for Assessment: Checklists, Rubrics,
    and Rating Scales   19
    Checklists   19

What Is a Checklist?	19
When Might We Use a Checklist?	20
How Do We Construct a Checklist?	20
How Do We Use a Checklist to Assess for Information Literacy?	21
Rubrics	21
What Is a Rubric?	21
When Might We Use a Rubric?	22
How Do We Construct an Instructional Rubric?	23
How Do We Use Rubrics to Assess for Information Literacy?	25
Rating Scales	27
What Is a Rating Scale?	27
When Might We Use a Rating Scale?	27
How Do We Construct a Rating Scale?	27
How Do We Use a Rating Scale to Assess for Information Literacy?	28
Conclusion	28
References	29
Chapter 4 Tools for Assessments: Conferences, Logs, and Personal Correspondence	31
Conferences	31
What Is a Conference?	31
When Might We Use Conferences to Assess Learning?	31
How Do We Structure the Conference?	33
How Do We Use Conferences to Assess for Information Literacy?	33
Logs	35
What Is a Log?	35
When Might We Use Logs as Assessment Tools?	36
How Do We Facilitate the Use of Logs?	38
How Do We Use Logs to Assess for Information Literacy?	40
Personal Correspondence	44
What Is Personal Correspondence?	44
When Might We Use Personal Correspondence to Assess Learning?	44
How Do We Construct the Correspondence?	44
How Do We Use Personal Correspondence to Assess for Information Literacy?	46
Conclusion	48
References	48

Chapter 5   Tools for Assessment: Graphic Organizers   49
             What Are Graphic Organizers?   49
             Concept Maps   50
                 What Is a Concept Map?   50
                 When Might We Use a Concept Map?   50
                 How Do We Construct a Concept Map?   52
                 How Do We Use a Concept Map to Assess
                     for Information Literacy?   52
             Webs   56
                 What Is a Web?   56
                 When Might We Use a Web?   56
                 How Do We Construct a Web?   57
                 How Do We Use a Web to Assess
                     for Information Literacy?   57
             K-W-L Charts   59
                 What Is a K-W-L Chart?   59
                 When Might We Use a K-W-L Chart?   59
                 How Do We Construct a K-W-L Chart?   60
                 How Do We Use a K-W-L (or K-W-H-L)
                     Chart to Assess for Information Literacy?   61
             Matrices   63
                 What Is a Matrix?   63
                 When Might We Use a Matrix?   63
                 How Do We Construct a Matrix?   63
                 How Do We Use a Matrix to Assess
                     for Information Literacy?   64
             Conclusion   66
             References   67

Chapter 6   Beginning with the End in Mind: Elementary
             Grade Example   68
             Outcome-Based Approach   68
             Summary of Project   69
             Sample Lessons   70
                 Lesson 1: Finding Information in a Variety
                     of Sources   70
                     Outcomes Desired   70
                         Standards and Performance
                             Indicators Addressed   70
                         Learning Task Related to Performance Indicator   70
                     Assessment   70
                         Criteria for Assessment   70
                         Tool or Method for Assessment   73
                     Instructional Procedure   73

                    Lesson 2: Developing Criteria to Assess
                        Student Books   73
                        Outcomes Desired   73
                            Standards and Performance
                                Indicators Addressed   73
                            Learning Task Related to Performance
                                Indicator   73
                        Assessment   73
                            Criteria for Assessment   73
                            Tool or Method for Assessment   76
                        Instructional Procedure   76
                    Conclusion   76
                    References   80

Chapter 7   Beginning with the End in Mind: Middle
             School Example   81
             Summary of Project   81
             Sample Lessons   82
                    Lesson 1: Asking the Right Questions   82
                        Outcomes Desired   82
                            Standards and Performance
                                Indicators Addressed   82
                            Learning Task Related to
                                Performance Indicator   82
                        Assessment   82
                            Criteria for Assessment   82
                            Tool or Method for Assessment   83
                        Instructional Procedure   84
                    Lesson 2: Appreciating Creative Forms
                        of Expression   86
                        Outcomes Desired   86
                            Standards and Performance
                                Indicators Addressed   86
                            Learning Task Related to
                                Performance Indicator   86
                        Assessment   87
                            Criteria for Assessment   87
                            Tool or Method for Assessment   88
                        Instructional Procedure   88
                    Conclusion   88
                    References   91

Chapter 8   Beginning with the End in Mind: High
             School Example   92
             Summary of Project   93

Sample Lessons   93
    Lesson 1: Evaluating Web Sites   94
        Outcomes Desired   94
            Standards and Performance
                Indicators Addressed   94
            Learning Task Related to Performance Indicator   95
        Assessment   95
            Criteria for Assessment   95
            Tool or Method for Assessment   95
        Instructional Procedure   96
    Lesson 2: Preparing an Annotated Bibliography   100
        Outcomes Desired   100
            Standards and Performance
                Indicators Addressed   100
            Learning Task Related to
                Performance Indicator   100
        Assessment   100
            Criteria for Assessment   100
            Tool or Method for Assessment   101
        Instructional Procedure   101
    Conclusion   101
    References   105

Chapter 9   Student Portfolios   106
    What Is a Portfolio?   106
    What Is an Electronic Portfolio?   106
    How Do Portfolios Differ from
        Other Assessment Tools?   107
    Why Use Portfolios?   108
    Who Are the Audiences for Portfolios?   109
    How Might the Library Media Specialist Use Portfolios?   110
    What Might a Process Folio Include?   110
        Step 1: Determine Standards That Are
            the Focus for Instruction and Assessment   111
        Step 2: Develop Tools and Strategies
            to Assess Achievement of Each Standard   112
        Step 3: Devise a Consistent Rating System
            for Assessment Tools Used   112
            Example A: Matrix for Identifying Resources   113
            Example B: Checklist for Bookmaking   114
        Step 4: Identify Samples of Student Work
            to Include for Each Standard   114
            Sample Work A: Completed Matrix   114
            Sample Work B: Completed Checklist   114

Step 5: Include Samples of Student Reflections   116
Step 6: Prepare a Summary Sheet
    for the Process Folio   120
Getting Started   122
Conclusion   122
References   123
Additional Readings on E-Portfolios   124

Chapter 10   Communicating Evidence of Learning   125
How Can Assessment Data Be Used to
    Support School-Wide Goals?   126
Why Is It Important to Communicate Results?   126
Communicating with Teachers   127
Step 1: Collect Evidence of Achievement   127
Step 2: Analyze Evidence   129
Step 3: Synthesize Findings   129
Step 4: Communicate Results   131
Communicating with Principals and School Councils   131
Step 1: Collect Evidence of Achievement   132
Step 2: Analyze Evidence   133
Step 3: Synthesize Findings   134
Step 4: Communicate Results   136
Communicating with the Larger Community   137
Step 1: Collect Evidence of Achievement   137
Step 2: Analyze Evidence   138
Step 3: Synthesize Findings   140
Step 4: Communicate Results   141
Conclusion   143
References   144

Index   145

Illustrations

1.1 Linear model of relationships among curriculum, instruction, and evaluation   2

1.2 Dynamic model of relationships among curriculum, instruction, and assessment   2

1.3 Moving from a focus on resources to student learning   6

2.1 Grade 7 unit: Integrating information literacy skills in authentic learning   12

2.2 Matching assessment methods with tools for recording information   14

2.3 Grade 7 unit: Matching assessment methods with information literacy standards   15

2.4 Relationship between standards and assessment   16

2.5 Grade 7 unit: Example of backward planning   17

3.1 Questions used to create an observation checklist   20

3.2 Checklist for assessing efficient and effective access to information   22

3.3 Steps in creating a rubric   24

3.4 Rubric for note taking   26

3.5 Evidence to assess instructional targets for Bill of Rights unit   28

3.6 Rating scale for assessing targeted aspects of the research process   29

4.1 Linking conferencing questions with instructional targets   33

4.2 Matching journal prompts with information literacy goals   36

4.3 Learning log for primary research projects   38

4.4 Example of synthesis log A   39

4.5 Example of synthesis log B   39

4.6   Example of literary response log   39
4.7   Prompts for assessing aspects of information literacy   41
4.8   Using letters and notes to assess instructional goals   45
4.9   Template for invitation to a science fair   45
4.10   Template for parents' response   46
4.11   Notes and letters used to assess the information
       literacy process   47

5.1   Examples of organizers for different learning objectives   51
5.2   Steps in constructing a concept map   53
5.3   Concept map for the rain forest ecosystem   54
5.4   Concept map for howler monkey   55
5.5   Web for "How did the colonists live?"   58
5.6   Web showing contributions made by colonial tradespeople   58
5.7   Using the K-W-L chart to organize the research process   60
5.8   Basic K-W-L chart   60
5.9   K-W-H-L chart   61
5.10   K-W-H-L chart for pet project   62
5.11   Model for constructing a comparison matrix   64
5.12   Matrix for comparing candidates and issues   65

6.1   Conventional versus outcome-based planning   68
6.2   Standards and performance indicators addressed in lesson 1   71
6.3   Criteria for locating and using a variety of sources   72
6.4   Matrix for identifying resources   72
6.5   Instructional procedure for identifying information sources   74
6.6   Map of library resources   75
6.7   Standards and performance indicators addressed in lesson 2   75
6.8   Criteria for evaluating student books   76
6.9   Checklist for assessing Wetlands books   77
6.10   Instructional procedure for developing assessment
       criteria with students   78
6.11   Grade 3 project: Focus, outcome, task, and assessment tool   80

7.1   Standards and performance indicators addressed in lesson 1   83
7.2   Criteria for questions   83
7.3   Assessment rubric for generating questions   84
7.4   Instructional procedure for lesson on generating questions   85

7.5   Standards and performance indicators addressed in lesson 2   87
7.6   Criteria for deriving meaning from information presented
      in different formats   88
7.7   Tool for responding to literature in multiple formats
      and genres   89
7.8   Instructional procedure for responding to creative forms of
      expression   90
7.9   Grade 8 unit: Focus, outcome, task, and assessment tool   91

8.1   Standards and performance indicators addressed in lesson 1   94
8.2   Criteria for evaluating web sites   95
8.3   Tool for assessing web sites   96
8.4   Instructional procedure for evaluating web sites   97
8.5   Standards and performance indicators addressed in lesson 2 100
8.6   Criteria for assessing annotated bibliographies   101
8.7   Rubric for assessing annotated bibliographies   102
8.8   Instructional procedure for developing bibliographies   103
8.9   Senior project: Focus, outcome, task, and assessment tool   104

9.1   Portfolios versus other assessment measures   108
9.2   Use of portfolios by different audiences   109
9.3   Standards and assessment measures for Wetlands unit   112
9.4   Matrix for identifying resources   113
9.5   Rating system for matrix   114
9.6   Checklist for assessing Wetlands books   115
9.7   Rating system for checklist   116
9.8   Example of student-completed matrix
      for identifying resources   117
9.9   Example of student-completed checklist for assessing
      Wetlands books   118
9.10 Example of student log for the Wetlands unit   120
9.11 Example of student's summary sheet for the Wetlands unit   121

10.1 Steps involved in evidence-based assessment   126
10.2 Matrix for identifying resources (work sample)   128
10.3 Rubric for assessing the resource matrix (assessment tool) 129
10.4 Sample of grade 3 class profile   130
10.5 Alignment of standards and performance indicators
      for reading and information literacy   132

10.6   Literature response form   133

10.7   Tool for assessing responses to literature   134

10.8   Sample of grade 8 class profile   135

10.9   Profile of achievement   136

10.10   Sample of tally sheet   138

10.11   Plan for presentation   139

10.12   Synthesizing data about the use of technology   140

10.13   Synthesizing data related to technology use   141

10.14   Percentage of students using technology
        to locate information   142

10.15   Percentage of students using technology
        to present information   143

10.16   Student attitudes toward technology   143

Acknowledgments

We extend our gratitude to Sharon Coatney, Acquisitions Editor at Libraries Unlimited, for encouraging us to develop this book and for providing constructive feedback through the production of this manuscript.

We also express our warmest aloha to our fellow library media specialists and teachers in Hawaii and across the nation, who have helped us shape our vision and thinking about the issue of assessment for learning. We also have the deepest appreciation for the wisdom shared by so many library educators, who have been professional colleagues imparting both inspiration and insight on this topic.

Finally, we thank our spouses Byron and Wayne for their continuous encouragement and wholehearted support.

Introduction

"I have to teach the same skills year after year because the students don't seem to get them."

"I don't have time to give students quizzes and tests so I can't really assess their work."

"Assessment is not my responsibility because I don't grade the students. It's the teacher's job."

"My job is getting kids excited about reading and helping them with their research, not conducting assessment."

"My goal is producing lifelong learners. That is a long-term goal. It happens in the future and you can't assess these skills now."

MYTHS

Do these remarks sound familiar? We have heard variations of these comments repeated at meetings, workshops, conferences, and informal gatherings wherever library media specialists have a chance to network and exchange "war stories." Let's revisit these comments for a moment and discuss some of the underlying myths that support them.

- *"I have to teach the same skills year after year because the students don't seem to get them."*

  Myth 1: The fault lies with students, who are simply unable to learn.

  Myth 2: Addressing these skills necessitates teaching them in the same way over and over again. Repetition rather than assessment and modification of teaching strategies is the most effective way to achieve more effective student learning.

- *"I don't have time to give them quizzes and tests so I can't really assess their work."*

  Myth 3: The primary method of assessing student performance is through the administration of traditional evaluation instruments, such as paper and pencil tests.

- *"Assessment is not my responsibility because I don't grade the students. It's the teacher's job."*

  Myth 4: Assessment and evaluation are one and the same. Since library media specialists don't usually give grades, they also don't assess students' work.

- *"My job is getting kids excited about reading and helping them with their research, not conducting assessment."*

  Myth 5: Skills and attitudes that help students develop their abilities to read and use information do not require assessment.

- *"My goal is producing lifelong learners. That is a long-term goal. It happens in the future and you can't assess these skills now."*

  Myth 6: Developing skills and dispositions for lifelong learning are *not* the focus of instruction in the library. These are attributes that learners somehow acquire (on their own) later in life.

If these myths actually drive current practices in the library media profession, we need to seriously rethink them. In today's schools, assessment for student learning is every school professional's business. With the publication of national standards for information literacy (AASL and AECT 1998), library media specialists have a research-based foundation for what is taught in school libraries. Sharon Coatney (2003), former president of the American Association of School Librarians, also emphasizes that assessment needs to be multifaceted (2003, 157), covering a range of standards-based indicators and using various tools and strategies to assess learning in K-12 settings.

If our goal is to engage students in ways that help them grow into confident, self-directed adult learners, we must demonstrate how our teaching contributes to this development. Not only is it critical to teach the *how to* but it is equally crucial to measure *how well* students demonstrate their learning. Library media specialists are involved in daily assessment of many kinds but there is a real need to conduct ongoing assessment of student progress and to report it in a manner that communicates the results to school staff, students, and parents (Kansas Association of School Librarians 2001).

CHALLENGES

There is no doubt that library media specialists face real challenges in today's schools (Neuman 2000):

- Administrators and teachers have not fully accepted the increased instructional role of the library media specialist.
- Library media specialists themselves may be reluctant to assume this role.
- Additional training is essential for library media specialists to assess student outcomes in information literacy.

These challenges point to the fact that effecting change in the school is a complex endeavor. Making the transition is not an overnight process.

Grover and colleagues describe this as a formidable undertaking likened to eating an elephant (Kansas Association of School Librarians 2001). One does it, a bite at a time.

For library media specialists, a critical first bite is orienting themselves to the purposes of assessment and learning about possible strategies to develop their own assessment tools. This book focuses on these major targets. It is based on the following core beliefs:

- Assessment is a critical tool to help students determine their strengths and weaknesses and work on improvements.
- Assessment is an equally valuable means of analyzing and informing instruction.
- Assessment is *not* evaluation; it is infused throughout the learning and teaching experience rather than limited to final outcomes.
- Assessment is not an add-on; it is integral to effective teaching and learning.

ORGANIZATION OF BOOK

This book is organized as follows:

Chapter 1 provides a context for assessment in today's schools.

Chapter 2 examines the role of the library media specialist as a partner in assessment.

Chapters 3 through 5 describe various tools for assessing student learning in the library media center and provide examples of their uses in integrated classroom-library instruction.

Chapters 6 through 8 illustrate how teachers and library media specialists at the elementary, middle, and high schools might collaborate on units that are based on standards and desired learning outcomes.

Chapter 9 delineates how library media specialists might work with teachers on portfolio assessment.

Chapter 10 explores how assessment data might be organized and shared with various stakeholder groups in a school community.

Library media specialists are vital partners in teaching. Their physical classrooms are their library media centers; however, their virtual learning centers extend to information and knowledge in the global community. As instructors, they need to ask themselves the following questions:

- What exactly does a lifelong learner do?
- How do we help to produce such learners?
- How can we prove that our teaching has made a difference?

This book invites library media specialists to delve into these questions and find meaningful answers that help them build a compelling case for the power of classroom-library partnerships for learning.

REFERENCES

American Association of School Librarians and Association for Educational Communications and Technology. 1998. *Information Power: Building Partnerships for Learning*. Chicago, Ill.: American Library Association.

Coatney, Sharon. 2003. "Assessment for Learning." In *Curriculum Connections Through the Library*, ed. Barbara K. Stripling and Sandra Hughes-Hassell. Westport, Conn.: Libraries Unlimited, pp. 157–68.

Kansas Association of School Librarians. Research Committee. 2001. *The Handy 5: Planning and Assessing Integrated Information Skills Instruction*, ed. Robert Grover, Carol Fox, and Jacqueline M. Lakin. Lanham, Md.: Scarecrow Press.

CHAPTER 1

Assessment in Today's School

This chapter addresses the following essential questions:

- What is assessment?
- What's happening with assessment in our schools?
- How does *No Child Left Behind* impact assessment?
- Do effective library media programs make a difference in student learning?
- What is the library media specialist's role in assessing student learning?

WHAT IS ASSESSMENT?

Assessment is the process of "collecting, analyzing, and reporting data" that informs both student and instructor of the progress and the problems that the student encounters throughout a learning experience (Coatney 2003, 157). It differs from evaluation in that assessment is conducted as an ongoing activity that provides crucial *formative* information about what the student is learning and how that learning is taking place. Students compare their performance against established criteria; they know what is expected before they begin their work (Donham 1998). In contrast, evaluation is a *summative* activity that occurs at the end of a learning experience. Its primary intent is to place a value on the student's performance.

WHAT'S HAPPENING WITH ASSESSMENT IN OUR SCHOOLS?

For almost two decades, assessment has been the intense focus of our nation's educational reform agenda. Rather than viewing curriculum, instruction, and assessment as having a linear relationship, the current perspective emphasizes an interactive, dynamic relationship among these three key elements. The contrastive models are depicted in Figures 1.1 and 1.2.

Cognitive learning theory and its constructivist approach to knowledge acquisition supports this dynamic process. In this model, assessment is fully integrated with instructional outcomes and curriculum content (Herman et al. 1992). This interactive concept of assessment is part of a larger paradigm shift in which learning and understanding are seen as a spiraling, student-focused process. In this process, assessment becomes critical in reshaping and reordering knowledge through action and reflection. The aim of assessment

Figure 1.1
Linear model of relationships among curriculum, instruction, and evaluation

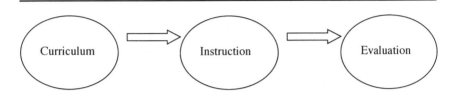

Figure 1.2
Dynamic model of relationships among curriculum, instruction, and assessment

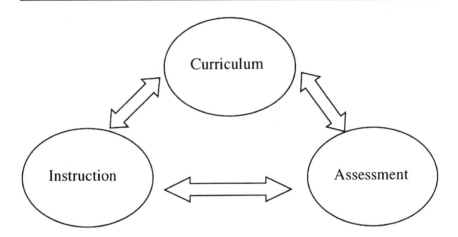

becomes *educating and improving* student performance, not merely *auditing* it (Wiggins 1998).

If we view assessment as this type of *learning tool* that serves both the instructor and student, there are two important underlying assumptions:

Students Must Be Central Partners in Assessment

By participating in assessment, students figure out what they are doing and where they are heading. Emerging brain research supports learning theories that propose we interpret the world through our mental models (Pinker 1997). Therefore it is important to involve students from the beginning to help them shape anticipatory mental models of their learning. When students participate in the assessment process, they develop the following behaviors (Chappuis and Stiggins 2002):

- Students understand what is expected.
- They access prior knowledge.

- They have ownership over making the learning happen.
- They are able to give themselves, as well as others, descriptive feedback as they are learning.
- Assessment goes beyond *measuring*; it becomes *motivating*.

Teachers Must View Assessment as Integral and Ongoing

Teachers must not view assessment as "an *add on* to the curriculum, something to be squeezed in, something for which time must be found. It must be seen as *a part* of pedagogy rather than *apart* from it" (Adkison and Tchudi 2000, 3–4). Seen in this light, assessment is an indispensable tool to inform and strengthen teaching. It is integrated throughout the instruction rather than limited to final outcomes. It takes place consistently and constantly. It becomes *a tool for learning and teaching* (Guskey 2003).

HOW DOES *NO CHILD LEFT BEHIND* IMPACT ASSESSMENT?

The landmark authorization of the No Child Left Behind (NCLB) Act represented a sweeping overhaul of federal support for K-12 education in the United States based on schools meeting national and state content standards. NCLB requires that states implement comprehensive accountability systems covering all students in the public schools. It also requires annual testing of students against state standards in reading, mathematics, and science. Coatney (2003) makes a critical point that such testing has its place in "sorting and ranking schools, defining school improvement goals, and if used correctly, helping monitor and ensure school quality" (158). The individual states are responsible for determining their own tests and ensuring that these tests are aligned with the state's curriculum standards. Eisenberg (2004) indicates that districts and states should take the initiative to show the relationship between information literacy skills instruction and student performance on these tests. They can do this by conducting an item analysis to determine the test's alignment with information literacy instruction (Eisenberg 2004).

Coatney maintains that this type of large-scale testing is usually "not very helpful in determining *individual student needs* or informing students about their *progress on specific learning goals*" (158). The upshot is that while standardized tests figure prominently in NCLB, this federal initiative also necessitates that assessment programs include *multiple measures* to appraise students' higher-order thinking skills (Education Commission of the States 2002).

Given that NCLB acknowledges learning as a complex and variegated process, a variety of assessment tools must be administered so that the results can be triangulated to assure reliable data (Farmer 2003).

Authentic assessment of performance in the classroom and the library media center is a critical measurement of students' achievement and motivation (Callison 2003). In short, a balance between standardized tests for *accountability* purposes and school level assessment for *improved teaching and learning* in the classrooms offers students a powerful way to demonstrate mastery of content, skills, and dispositions essential to their success in the larger community (Partnership for 21st Century Skills 2003).

DO EFFECTIVE LIBRARY MEDIA PROGRAMS MAKE A DIFFERENCE?

There is a growing body of research that indicates effective library media programs positively impact student achievement. Among the most widely cited research have been the numerous studies undertaken by Keith Curry Lance and colleagues (cited in Todd 2003a). These surveys, involving hundreds of primary and secondary schools in Colorado, Alaska, Pennsylvania, New Mexico, Oregon, and Texas, have sought to empirically establish the relationship of school library programs to student achievement. One common finding across these surveys has been that professionally trained library media specialists positively affect students' performance on achievement tests.

Students themselves voiced overwhelming support for school library media centers as powerful sources for learning in a survey commissioned by the Ohio Educational Library Media Association (Whelan 2004). Ross Todd and Carol Kuhlthau of Rutgers University's Center for International Scholarship in School Libraries conducted the study, which involved over 13,000 students in grades 3 to 12. Over 90 percent of the student respondents indicated that use of computers in the school library media centers improved their overall academic work. They also noted that instruction in the libraries helped them get better grades on projects and assignments (88.5 percent) and assisted them with homework (74.7 percent).

In the international arena, the Council for Museums, Archives and Libraries in Scotland has conducted equally critical research on the impact of libraries on learning (Williams and Wavell 2001). This investigation provides evidence that school libraries positively influence a range of critical areas in the acquisition of information, including locating and using information, applying computer technology, strengthening reading comprehension, and developing study habits that encourage independent learning.

Library media specialists, as advocates for literacy and learning, must be active consumers of this research. They must have current knowledge of what the research is saying and how this research might help them improve their local situations. There are many avenues to access this information. Loertscher and Woolls (2002), Farmer (2003), Haycock (1999), and Thomas (1999) have compiled useful research summaries. *School Library*

Media Research (http://www.ala.org/aasl/slmr) provides online access to current research. *Teacher Librarian* highlights findings from dissertation studies and *Knowledge Quest* has a column dedicated to research impacting library media centers. *SCAN*, an Australian journal, and *School Libraries Worldwide*, edited by the International Association of School Librarianship, regularly publish research on the impact of library programs. These timely sources provide a rich compendium of information that can help library media specialists develop research-based practices.

WHAT IS THE LIBRARY MEDIA SPECIALIST'S ROLE?

While national and international studies regarding the impact of libraries on student achievement are important to the field, the *real evidence is often at the local level*. Todd (2003b) maintains that principals and parents "want to hear of local successes . . . they want to know how their students in particular are benefiting" (14). This requires that library media specialists actively participate in collecting this evidence.

The current national guidelines for school library media centers, *Information Power: Building Partnerships for Learning* (AASL and AECT 1998), envisions library media centers transitioning from a focus on providing resources to an emphasis on creating a community of lifelong learners. This transition requires that library media specialists view their "curriculum" as extending beyond the traditional location and retrieval skills to skills in evaluating, synthesizing, and interpreting information. It necessitates that a focus on completion of products be tempered with an equal emphasis on the process of learning. Importantly, it requires that library media specialists expand their data collection beyond the tabulation of quantitative statistics on collection size and circulation to measures of actual student learning. In short, it means shifting *mind-sets* from a concentration on *things* to a focus on *students*. Assessment becomes a shared responsibility with the classroom teacher. Figure 1.3 summarizes the paradigm shifts involved.

Benefits of Assessment

Students grow as learners when they participate in the assessment process. They become aware that the library media center and the classroom are part of the larger learning community with mutual targets and expectations. Students gain the following benefits:

- They are clearer about learning targets because the library media specialist is communicating learning expectations up front.
- They are more keenly motivated to learn because they know what is expected and how they can participate in the assessment of their own learning.

Figure 1.3
Moving from a focus on resources to student learning

Focus on Providing Resources	Focus on Student Learning
Teach skills that involve location and retrieval of library resources.	Teach skills that involve evaluation, synthesis, and interpretation of information.
Emphasize product.	Emphasize process as well as product.
Measure effectiveness through data on library's collection size, circulation, etc.	Measure effectiveness through how well students meet learning objectives.
View assessment as evaluating products, giving final grades.	View assessment as an ongoing examination of learning.
Believe that assessment is solely the responsibility of the teacher.	Believe that assessment is a shared responsibility with the teacher.

There are equally important benefits for the teacher and the library media specialist that are borne out by the research:

- Both instructors have a *map* for planning curriculum and instructional activities. They know more specifically what they hope to accomplish and have criteria to describe the outcomes expected. Thus assessment itself becomes an instructional activity (Asp 1998).
- When instructors assess for learning, positive changes happen. They include more opportunities for peer learning and collaboration, more choices for students in the learning environment, more integrated and interdisciplinary teaching, and increased use of learning contexts that stretch beyond the walls of the school (Falk 2000).
- Library media specialists, who are active in curriculum planning and instruction, provide support in specific areas of higher order thinking that include the skills and processes students need to access resources and information, think about ideas, and create their own approaches to information-related problems (Tallman 1995).
- For the library media specialists, documentation of the assessment results provides a compelling case for the value of the library program. When issues of funding accountability arise and decision makers identify priorities for staffs and budgets based on programs that *show student improvement*, library media specialists can produce student-focused data to support their requests.

Essential Questions for the Library Media Specialist

The following questions are critical ones for library media specialists seeking to assess the learning that occurs in their programs.

- What difference does my library media program make to students and their learning?
- What does this learning look like?
- What is the student able to do? What does the student know?
- How do I assess this learning?
- How do I organize and communicate this assessment data?

In the ensuing chapters, the authors grapple with these same questions that are essential for assessing a dynamic program for learning.

CONCLUSION

No one can provide a "one size fits all" formula for designing and implementing valid and reliable assessments that can be used for all curricula and all students. The individual school community must craft assessment tools and strategies for students' mastery of information literacy in their own school setting (Neuman 2000). As members of the school community, library media specialists have an opportunity to join the action and provide evidence of their best practices that contribute to high-quality learning in their schools.

Todd (2002) makes a thoughtful and eloquent case for the importance of assessment as the key to "evidence based practice":

The hallmark of a school library in the 21st century is not the teacher-librarian, nor its collections, systems, technology, staffing, or buildings (although we would all acknowledge that these, however, are critical). It is *actions* and *evidences* that show what makes a real difference to student learning, and that the teacher-librarian contributes in tangible and significant ways to the development of human understanding, meaning making and constructing knowledge. (35)

REFERENCES

Adkison, Stephen, and Stephen Tchudi. 2000. "Assessing Growth in English and the Language Arts: The Case for Evaluation as Pedagogy." In *Assessing Student Learning: A Practical Guide* [CD-ROM], ed. Kent Seidel. Cincinnati, Ohio: Alliance for Curriculum Reform.

American Association of School Librarians, and Association for Educational Communications and Technology. 1998. *Information Power: Building Partnerships for Learning*. Chicago, Ill.: American Library Association.

Asp, Elliott. 1998. "The Relationship Between Large-Scale and Classroom Assessment: Compatibility or Conflict?" In *Assessing Student Learning: New Rules, New Realities*, ed. Ron Brandt. Arlington, Va.: Educational Research Service, pp. 17–46.

Callison, Daniel. 2003. *Key Words, Concepts and Methods for Information Age Instruction: A Guide to Teaching Information Inquiry*. Baltimore, Md.: LMS Associates.

Chappuis, Stephen, and Richard J. Stiggins. 2002. "Classroom Assessment for Learning," *Educational Leadership* 60, no. 1 (September): 40–43.

Coatney, Sharon. 2003. "Assessment for Learning." In *Curriculum Connections Through the Library*, ed. Barbara K. Stripling and Sandra Hughes-Hassell. Westport, Conn.: Libraries Unlimited, pp. 157–68.

Donham, Jean. 1998. *Assessment of Information Processes and Products*. Chicago, Ill.: Follett Software Co.

Education Commission of the States. 2002. *No State Left Behind: The Challenges and Opportunities of ESEA 2001*. Washington, D.C.: Author. URL: http://www.ecs. org/html/Special/ESEA/NSLBmain.htm (accessed December 22, 2003).

Eisenberg, Michael B. 2004. "It's All About Learning: Ensuring That Students Are Effective Users of Information on Standardized Tests," *Library Media Connection* 22, no. 6 (March): 22–30.

Falk, Beverly. 2000. *The Heart of the Matter: Using Standards and Assessment to Learn*. Portsmouth, N.H.: Heinemann.

Farmer, Lesley S.J. 2003. *Student Success and Library Media Programs: A Systems Approach to Research and Best Practice*. Westport, Conn.: Libraries Unlimited.

Guskey, Thomas R. 2003. "How Classroom Assessments Improve Learning," *Educational Leadership* 60, no. 5 (February): 6–11.

Haycock, Ken. 1999. *Foundations of Effective School Library Media Programs*. Englewood, Colo.: Libraries Unlimited.

Herman, Joan L., Pamela R. Aschbacker, and Lynn Winters. 1992. *A Practical Guide to Alternative Assessment*. Alexandria, Va.: Association for Supervision and Curriculum Development.

Loertscher, David V., and Blanche Woolls. 2002. *Information Literacy: A Review of the Research*. San Jose, Ca.: Hi Willow Research & Publishing.

Neuman, Delia. 2000. "Information Power and Assessment: The Other Side of the Standards Coin." In *Educational Media and Technology Yearbook*, ed. Robert M. Branch and Mary Ann Fitzgerald. Englewood, Colo.: Libraries Unlimited, pp. 110–19.

Partnership for 21st Century Skills. 2003. *Learning for the 21st Century: A Report and MILE Guide for 21st Century Skills*. Washington, D.C.: Author.

Pinker, Steven. 1997. *How the Mind Works*. New York: HarperCollins.

Tallman, Julie I. 1995. "Curriculum Consultation: Strengthening Activity Through Multiple-Content Area Units," *School Library Media Quarterly* 24, no. 1 (Fall): 27–34.

Thomas, Nancy P. 1999. *Information Literacy and Information Skills Instruction: Applying Research to Practice in the School Library Media Center*. Englewood, Colo.: Libraries Unlimited.

Todd, Ross J. 2002. "Evidence Based Practice II: Getting into the Action," *SCAN* 21, no. 2 (May): 34–41.

Todd, Ross J. 2003a. "Evidence Based Practice: Overview, Rationale, and Challenges." In *We Can Boost Achievement! Evidence-Based Practice for School Library Media Specialists*, ed. David V. Loertscher. Salt Lake City, Utah: Hi Willow Research & Publishing, pp. 1–24.

Todd, Ross J. 2003b. "School Libraries Evidence: Seize the Day, Begin the Future," *Library Media Connection* 22, no. 1 (August/September): 12–17.

Whelan, Debra L. 2004. "13,000 Kids Can't Be Wrong," *School Library Journal* 50, no. 2 (February): 46–50. URL: http://www.schoollibraryjournal.com/index. asp?layout=articlePrint&articleID=CA377858 (accessed May 24, 2004).

Wiggins, Grant. 1998. *Educative Assessment: Designing Assessments to Inform and Improve Student Performance.* San Francisco, Ca.: Jossey-Bass.

Williams, Dorothy A., and Caroline Wavell. 2001. *The Impact of the School Library Resource Centre on Learning. Library and Information Commission Research Report 112.* Aberdeen, Scotland: Robert Gordon University.

CHAPTER 2

Assessment in the Library Media Center

This chapter addresses the following questions:

- What do we assess?
- How do we assess for learning?
- What are the necessary first steps?

WHAT DO WE ASSESS?

Authentic Learning

As schools focus on standards-based teaching and learning, educators are grappling with the challenge of devising instruction that involves higher levels of thinking and problem solving. This type of learning is often referred to as authentic because it provides a meaningful context for the experience (Marzano et al. 2001, Mills and Donnelly 2001, Newmann et al. 1995). Such learning also presents students with a range of opportunities to demonstrate their newly acquired knowledge (Strickland and Strickland 2000). The tasks are multidimensional: they involve generating meaningful questions, collecting and analyzing information related to the questions, organizing the information to make an effective argument, and persuasively communicating all of this information to a real audience.

What might this type of learning look like? Here is an example.

> Seventh-grade students view a local television news special about trash becoming a serious problem in their community. This stimulates their curiosity and concern about the issue. They talk with neighbors and spend a few days surveying their own school campus and their neighborhoods to grasp the scope of the problem. In class, they decide they want to wrestle with the following overarching questions: How big a problem is trash in our community? Why has this become a serious problem? What can we do about this problem?
>
> They work with their teacher and the library media specialist to identify sources of information and collect data. In teams they

> create posters and leaflets based on their information and secure the cooperation of merchants at the community mall to display their posters and distribute the information. One group of students also produces a 90-second public service announcement that is aired on local television. Throughout the process, students reflect on their experiences and critique each other's works in progress.

Stripling (1999) identifies several ways in which authentic learning tasks such as the one just described support the goals of standards-based teaching:

- It requires students to construct their own knowledge. Authentic learning shifts the focus from memorizing and repeating facts to using information to develop ideas.
- The inquiry process is used as a model for the in-depth learning implicit in the standards.
- Students engage in a study of real-world problems and issues. They ask probing questions and gather information from a variety of sources available in different formats. The students evaluate, analyze, and interpret information in relation to the problem. They work with peers to produce products and to work on projects related to relevant problems or issues.
- This type of learning has value beyond the school environment. Students develop academic skills by working on real problems. In the process they acquire the knowledge, skills, and attitudes needed in a democratic society.

Information Literacy

A major contribution that library media specialists make to authentic learning situations is working with students to refine their skills in information seeking and use. The publishing of the Information Literacy Standards for Student Learning (AASL and AECT 1998) was a landmark accomplishment. For the first time, library media programs had research-based standards that gave library media specialists a legitimacy in the larger school reform movement (Doyle 1992, Neuman 2000).

The Information Literacy Standards are organized in three major clusters. The first cluster focuses on information literacy—the students' ability to access, evaluate, and use information. These skills are most "centrally related to the services provided by school library media programs" (AASL and AECT 1998, x). The other two clusters—independent learning and social responsibility—deal with more general concepts and skills that all school programs, including the library media center, should target. They include pursuing information that satisfies students' personal needs and interests, appreciating literature and other forms of creative expression, demonstrating ethical behavior in the use of print and electronic resources, and working effectively with others to accomplish common goals. These standards focus on higher order thinking skills that cut across all curricula (Harada 2003).

When the library media specialist works side-by-side with the classroom teacher, information skills instruction becomes a major vehicle for engaging students in meaningful learning. As students use an information search model to build knowledge, they are working toward achievement of the content standards as well as information literacy goals. What might the library media specialist contribute to a specific learning project? As an example, Figure 2.1 suggests how classroom and library reinforce critical skills in the seventh-grade scenario posed earlier in this chapter. In actual practice, the sample activities that are introduced in the classroom may be continued in the library media center or vice versa. The point is that the instructors work as a team to make the learning experience a dynamic and seamless one for the students.

Figure 2.1
Grade 7 unit: Integrating information literacy skills in authentic learning

Information seeking skills	In the classroom	In the library
Explore the problem or issue	View the television special on trash. Survey neighbors, explore campus and community	Skim through additional resources on the issue to gain an overview
Find a focus for the investigation	Develop essential questions	Brainstorm resources that might be used to answer questions
Plan the information search and presentation	Decide on ways to communicate information	Develop keyword searches for information
Evaluate and collect information	Take notes	Evaluate web sites
Organize and present information	Design and produce leaflets, posters, and public service announcements	Analyze need for additional information
Assess the process and presentations	Assess self-progress on preparing products	Assess self-progress throughout information search process

Relationship to Content Standards

Information literacy standards are an integral component of learning in any content area. As a process by which students access, retrieve, and critically use data to generate knowledge for themselves (Kuhlthau 2004), learning to be information literate is a requisite for mastering all disciplines. It is, therefore, critical to emphasize that teaching "information literacy skills" is not a "content-free" process. In fact, closer examination of various content standards reveals that information literacy competencies are embedded in them. *Information Power: Building Partnerships for Learning* (AASL and AECT 1998) provides examples of the link between various content and information literacy standards.

In language arts, for instance, students "must conduct research on issues and interests by generating ideas and questions, and by posing problems" (NCTE and IRA n.d., online). In science, students must develop "the abilities necessary to do scientific inquiry" (National Academy of Sciences n.d., online). In mathematics, students must "apply and adapt a variety of appropriate strategies to solve problems," and "develop and evaluate arguments and proofs" (National Council of Teachers of Mathematics 2000, online).

The critical point is that school library media specialists must seize the opportunity to show how our teaching reinforces and enhances classroom learning. By noting both the content as well as information literacy standards in our instructional plans, we make visible the synergistic relationship between student engagement in both the classroom and the library media center. The bottom line is that teachers need to see how the classroom-library partnership targets their own goals and priorities.

HOW DO WE ASSESS FOR LEARNING?

Since the advent of standards-based teaching and learning, teachers and library media specialists have experimented with different strategies for recording and analyzing assessment data. Figure 2.2 identifies some of the tools that might be used to assess student performance. They are categorized under three headings: observation, personal communication, and the examination of student work (Davies 2000).

To show how some of these tools or methods might be incorporated into a unit of study, we return to the seventh-grade project and outline possible ways to assess the achievement of standards in this specific unit (Figure 2.3).

In the next three chapters we present additional descriptions and examples of these various assessment tools. They are organized as follows:

- Chapter 3: Checklists, rubrics, and rating scales
- Chapter 4: Conferences, logs, and personal communication
- Chapter 5: Graphic organizers

Figure 2.2
Matching assessment methods with tools for recording information

Assessment Method	Tools for Recording Information
Observation	• **Checklists** list desired behaviors • **Rubrics** identify criteria for successful performance and describe different levels of performance • **Rating scales** place different levels of performance along a scale
Personal communication	• **Informal conferences** ask questions and probe for understanding • **Formal conferences** lead to insights into the student's learning process • **Logs** have students record their thoughts and feelings about the content and process • **Notes and letters** encourage students to self-assess and seek feedback
Examination of student work	• **Checklists** list criteria for proficiency • **Rubrics** describe various levels of proficiency • **Graphic organizers** allow students to organize and synthesize their information • **Portfolios** provide a cumulative view of students' learning by offering samples of work that are matched to curriculum goals (including information literacy standards)

WHAT ARE THE NECESSARY FIRST STEPS?

In assessment-focused instruction, library media specialists start with an idea of what the students must be able to do *at the end of the learning experience.* Wiggins and McTighe (1998) have popularized the term "backward design" (146) to describe this important concept in curriculum planning. Other educators (Perkins 1992, Wiske 1994, Mitchell et al. 1995, Luongo-Orlando 2003) have advocated similar approaches to instructional design. This type of planning challenges instructors to identify the outcomes first and the means by which outcomes will be measured before creating the activities themselves.

Figure 2.3
Grade 7 unit: Matching assessment methods with information literacy standards

Information literacy standard	Assessment method
Accesses information efficiently and effectively	***Observation*** of students' use of library resources Teachers and library media specialists (LMS) observe students as they access information. Questions are used to focus on specific behaviors. For example: • Does he or she have a search strategy? • Does he or she use a variety of print and electronic resources? • Does he or she follow protocols for accessing, selecting, and downloading information?
Evaluates information critically and competently	***Personal communication*** Teachers and LMS ask questions to determine how well the student evaluates information. For example: • Which resources are most likely to address your research questions? • What accounts for discrepancies in the information gathered from different sources? • How does this piece of information support your main idea or hypothesis?
Uses information accurately and creatively	***Examination of student work*** Teachers and LMS assess products and performance with a focus on desired outcomes. For example: • Does the product explain the extent of the problem and its impact on the community? • Is the message clear and to the point? • Is the content accurate? • Is the content documented?

Starting with a clear notion of the end applies not just to planning a unit of study; it should also be reflected in creating individual lessons. There are two critical questions involved in this process (Harada and Yoshina 2004):

• What must students be able to demonstrate or perform by the end of this experience?
• How can we measure how well students have achieved this goal?

The following steps are crucial in this type of planning:

• Begin by identifying the broad standard being addressed.
• Articulate a more specific performance indicator related to the standard.
• Describe a learning task based on the performance indicator. This may be referred to as a performance task.

- Determine the criteria that will be used to assess how well students perform the learning task.
- Design the tool or method to measure proficiency.

The following figure captures these steps in a visual form.

Figure 2.4
Relationship between standards and assessment

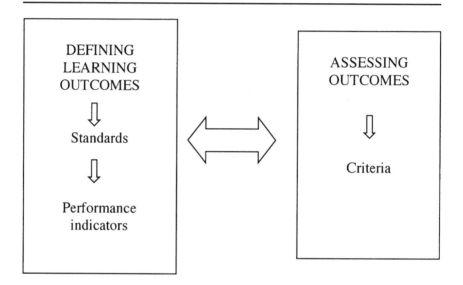

Figure 2.5 is an example of how backward planning is used for one of the lessons integrated into the seventh-grade project on trash.

Chapters 6 through 8 provide more detailed examples of how to apply this outcome-based approach to lessons conducted in the library media center.

CONCLUSION

As partners in teaching, library media specialists have a responsibility to provide evidence of the learning that results from their instruction. This instruction should be aligned with the standards and learning goals being targeted in the classrooms. No one instrument can adequately generate the evidence needed to assess any of the standards. The following are critical points to keep in mind:

- Students should be actively engaged in assessing their own learning.
- The purpose of the assessment is to gather information on the *how* as well as the *what* of learning.
- Assessment methods must be appropriately matched with the desired outcomes.

Figure 2.5
Grade 7 unit: Example of backward planning

Steps in Backward Planning	What It Looks Like
1. Identify the standard being addressed.	The student who is information literate accesses information efficiently and effectively.
2. Identify the performance indicator related to the standard.	The student develops and uses successful strategies for locating information.
3. Describe the learning task based on the performance indicator.	The student will develop a keyword search statement to access online information related to the essential questions.
4. Determine the criteria to assess student performance on the learning task.	In developing a keyword search statement, the student will be able to <ul><li>Identify keywords or phrases reflected in the questions</li><li>Identify appropriate synonyms for the keywords</li><li>Determine appropriate related terms</li></ul>
5. Design a tool or method to measure student proficiency.	The library media specialist creates a graphic organizer that includes spaces for the following items: <ul><li>Research question</li><li>Keywords or phrases in the question</li><li>Synonyms related to keywords or phrases</li><li>Related terms</li></ul> The completed graphic organizer will be used to assess student performance.

Importantly, the teachers and library media specialists work as partners with the students throughout the learning experiences. The critical purpose of gathering the information is not to grade a final product, but to provide the support and guidance needed for students to reach the highest levels of performance.

REFERENCES

American Association of School Librarians, and Association for Educational Communications and Technology. 1998. *Information Power: Building Partnerships for Learning*. Chicago, Ill.: American Library Association.

Davies, Anne. 2000. *Making Classroom Assessment Work*. British Columbia, Canada: Connections Publishing.

Doyle, Christina S. 1992. *Final Report to the National Forum on Information Literacy*. Syracuse, N.Y.: ERIC Clearinghouse on Information Resources. ED 351 033.

Harada, Violet H. 2003. "Empowered Learning: Fostering Thinking Across the Curriculum." In *Curriculum Connections Through the Library*, ed. Barbara K. Stripling and Sandra Hughes-Hassell. Westport, Conn.: Libraries Unlimited, pp. 41–65.

Harada, Violet H., and Joan M. Yoshina. 2004. *Inquiry Learning Through Librarian-Teacher Partnerships*. Worthington, Ohio: Linworth Publishing, Inc.

Kuhlthau, Carol. 2004. *Seeking Meaning: A Process Approach to Library and Information Services*. Westport, Conn.: Libraries Unlimited.

Luongo-Orlando, Katherine. 2003. *Authentic Assessment: Designing Performance-Based Tasks*. Ontario, Canada: Pembroke Publishers Limited.

Marzano, Robert J., Debra J. Pickering, and Jane E. Pollock. 2001. *Classroom Instruction That Works*. Alexandria, Va.: Association of Supervision and Curriculum Development.

Mills, Heidi, and Amy Donnelly. 2001. *From the Ground Up: Creating a Culture of Inquiry*. Portsmouth, N.H.: Heinemann.

Mitchell, Ruth, Marilyn Willis, and The Chicago Teachers Union Quest Center. 1995. *Learning in Overdrive: Designing Curriculum, Instruction, and Assessment from Standards*. Golden, Colo.: North American Press.

National Academy of Sciences. n.d. *National Science Education Standards*. URL: http://www.nap.edu/readingroom/books/nses/html/6d.html (accessed July 6, 2004).

National Council of Teachers of English, and International Reading Association. n.d. *Standards for the English Language Arts*. URL: http://www.ncte.org/about/over/standards/110846.htm (accessed July 6, 2004).

National Council of Teachers of Mathematics. 2000. *Principles and Standards for School Mathematics*. URL: http://www.standards.nctm.org/index.htm (accessed July 6, 2004).

Neuman, Delia. 2000. "Information Power and Assessment: The Other Side of the Standards Coin." In *Educational Media and Technology Yearbook*, ed. Robert. M. Branch and Mary Ann Fitzgerald. Englewood, Colo.: Libraries Unlimited, pp. 110–19.

Newmann, Fred M., Walter G. Secada, and Gary G. Wehlage. 1995. *A Guide to Authentic Instruction and Assessment: Vision, Standards and Scoring*. Madison, Wisc.: Wisconsin Center for Education Research.

Perkins, David N. 1992. *Smart Schools: From Training Memories to Educating Minds*. New York: Free Press.

Strickland, Kathleen, and James Strickland. 2000. *Making Assessment Elementary*. Portsmouth, N.H.: Heinemann.

Stripling, Barbara. 1999. "Expectations for Achievement and Performance: Assessing Student Skills," *NASSP Bulletin* 83, no. 605 (March): 44–52.

Wiggins, Grant, and Jay McTighe. 1998. *Understanding by Design*. Alexandria, Va.: Association for Supervision and Curriculum Development.

Wiske, Martha S. 1994. "How Teaching for Understanding Changes the Rules in the Classroom," *Educational Leadership* 51, no. 5 (February): 19–21.

CHAPTER 3

Tools for Assessment: Checklists, Rubrics, and Rating Scales

In this chapter, we look more closely at checklists, rubrics, and rating scales as tools for assessing student performance. The discussion for each tool is organized around the following key questions:

- What is it?
- When might we use this tool?
- How do we construct this tool?
- How do we use it to assess for information literacy?

To be used effectively, each of these tools requires that

- Criteria have been established to assess the quality of work in progress.
- Students are engaged in continuous use of the tools to gauge their own progress.
- Teachers and library media specialists examine the results to inform their own instruction.

CHECKLISTS

What Is a Checklist?

A checklist is a list of dimensions, characteristics, or behaviors needed for successful completion of the task. It can include criteria for both process and product. "Checklists are usually scored as 'yes-no' ratings. They do not tell you the *extent* to which behaviors are observed or the *quality* of the performance. They tell you only that a specified behavior was displayed" (Herman, Aschbacker, and Winters 1992, 64–65).

When it is given at the beginning of the assignment, students may use the checklist to guide them through the research process (Donham 1998). Teachers and library media specialists use checklists to focus their observations on critical aspects of the process.

When Might We Use a Checklist?

The checklist is especially useful as a tool for observing students as they work on projects involving several layers of learning. It is one way to lessen the subjectivity that often plagues more casual observations. Feedback and observation checklists are particularly helpful during cooperative learning projects, group presentations, and class discussions (Strickland and Strickland 2000). Checklists are also useful in conferencing with students because teachers can glance over the lists and quickly pick up where they left off at the last conference.

The checklist helps students as well as the teacher and library media specialist by focusing attention on important aspects of the task, for example:

- Students use the checklist at the outset to assess their abilities in terms of the requirements of the assignment and to get an overview of the entire process. At the completion of the task the same checklist is used to reflect on the learning process.
- Teachers and the library media specialist use the checklist as an instructional tool to focus attention on the requirements for a particular performance. The same checklist is used to provide feedback as students are working on the task and as a final assessment indicating whether criteria have been met.

In short, checklists keep instructors and students focused on what is important and they provide a record of student progress.

How Do We Construct a Checklist?

Checklists must be tailored to the requirements of the specific assignment. Figure 3.1 suggests questions that might be used to develop an observation checklist.

Figure 3.1
Questions used to create an observation checklist

- What standards do we need to assess?

- What are our instructional goals?

- How will students demonstrate their proficiency in meeting a standard?

- What are the observable or measurable indicators of success?

A well-constructed checklist has the following characteristics:

- It identifies behaviors that relate to the standards and the instructional goals.
- It focuses the observation on critical aspects of the task.
- It provides evidence linking student achievement with instructional goals.
- It can be used as an assessment tool by both students and instructors.

How Do We Use a Checklist to Assess for Information Literacy?

Grade 2 Scenario

Second graders are involved in a unit study about animal adaptation. The unit engages students in an inquiry cycle that begins with the selection of an animal from a particular habitat. The student asks questions related to the theme of adaptation and identifies resources that might answer those questions. The final task will be to create a riddle book that includes clues about the animal and a picture of the animal adapting to its habitat. After sharing their riddle books with research buddies, the students will display their books in the library media center so that other children can enjoy and respond to them.

The unit addresses content standards for reading, writing, oral communication, science, and visual arts. Evidence of learning is gathered through observation, conferencing, and the examination of student work. The library media specialist sees the project as an opportunity to teach and assess student achievement related to the first standard for information literacy: *The student who is information literate accesses information efficiently and effectively* (AASL and AECT 1998). Working with the teachers, he or she develops a checklist (Figure 3.2) to assess student performance. Students also use it to record their own perceptions about how they are learning.

RUBRICS

What Is a Rubric?

A rubric is an instrument that employs a grid design to define components of a task as well as gradations of their quality (Strickland and Strickland 2000). It identifies criteria for successful work and describes different levels or ranges of performance (Todd 2003, Callison 2003). Rubrics differ from other scoring guides in that they describe in detail the qualities that make a performance strong, adequate, or weak. A well-designed rubric

Figure 3.2
Checklist for assessing efficient and effective access to information

My tasks: I can....	Yes, I can do it.	No, I cannot do it yet.	Comments
Choose search words.			
Find a book in the online catalog.			
Use the call number to find a book.			
Use the table of contents to find my topic.			
Use the index to find the page.			
Find my topic in the electronic encyclopedia.			
Find my topic in a print encyclopedia.			
Find my topic on the Internet.			

is both a tool for assessment and a powerful teaching strategy. Although rubrics can take different formats, they have two characteristics in common:

- A list of criteria for a successful performance
- A description of varying levels of performance (Andrade 2000)

When Might We Use a Rubric?

Rubrics are best used to assess complex tasks, such as written compositions, projects and exhibits, and research assignments (Andrade 2000). Assessment of the information literacy standards engages students in authentic tasks that challenge them to think, problem solve, communicate, and demonstrate various skills ranging in complexity from asking questions that focus an inquiry to producing a product that demonstrates rigor, relevance, and creativity. Students might demonstrate their growing personal knowledge of the information literacy standards in the following ways:

- They employ an inquiry process to build personal knowledge about a subject.
- They access, evaluate, and use information from a variety of sources.
- They read and enjoy a range of literary genres including fiction, informational pieces, poetry, and traditional stories.
- They collaborate with others to create products and exhibitions that are useful to members of the community.

Stiggins (1997) has identified knowledge, reasoning, skills, products, and dispositions as instructional targets for which performance assessments would be appropriate. Clearly, all of these instructional goals are embedded in the information literacy standards. The trick is to define our instructional targets and to design a performance task through which each target can be assessed.

Since performance tasks require students to work independently and to monitor their own progress, the rubric can be used as a tool for instruction as well as assessment. By describing the elements of a successful performance, the rubric takes the guesswork out of learning. Students learn to use the rubric to self-assess as they work on different phases of the project.

How Do We Construct an Instructional Rubric?

Rubrics serve more than one purpose. Some are designed for teachers as tools for evaluation. These rubrics may use technical language not easily understood by students. This is in contrast to what Andrade (2000) calls an *instructional rubric*—one that is used for instruction as well as assessment. Since we believe that, to the extent possible, students should have a voice in deciding how their work will be assessed, we share the experiences we have had creating instructional rubrics with our students.

Designing and using instructional rubrics begins with involving students in a discussion of work samples that focus on the question "What makes good work?" The process includes brainstorming, discussion, and decision-making—all of which have the effect of engaging students in a serious conversation about quality. To create rubrics for our own projects, we have drawn from an instructional model developed by Heidi Goodrich Andrade (2000). Although there may be variations, the model generally includes the steps outlined in Figure 3.3.

Figure 3.3
Steps in creating a rubric

Steps in Creating a Rubric	What is Involved
Present models of student work.	Models may be anonymous samples of student work, videotapes of students working on a similar task, etc.
Discuss "What makes good work?"	In small groups students discuss which models represent the best work or the best performance and the qualities that make it best. Responses are noted on chart paper.
Explain the assignment and need for assessment criteria.	The teacher or library media specialist explains what students will be doing and relates the discussion of quality to the requirements of the assignment.
Discuss and select criteria for assessment.	Students review all of the charts and select no more than six criteria critical to successful performance in terms of the current assignment. (Limiting the number forces students to focus on what is most important.)
Draft a rubric.	The teacher and library media specialist draw upon the classroom discussion to create a rubric that identifies assessment criteria and describes different levels of performance.
Practice using the rubric.	Students practice using the rubric to assess work samples. Following the practice session, the rubric itself is assessed.
Revise the rubric.	Teachers and library media specialists draw upon students' comments and experience to revise the rubric.
Use the rubric to instruct, guide, and assess.	A revised copy of the rubric is given to each student. Students use it to self-assess and instructors use it to monitor progress.

How Do We Use Rubrics to Assess for Information Literacy?

Grade 8 Scenario

Eighth-grade students have identified "freedom" as a theme that runs throughout American history. They have learned that Europeans seeking freedom from poverty, oppression, and other forms of injustice fueled colonization in America. They are impressed with stories of the pioneers who crossed the continent at great personal risk to exercise their freedom of self-determination. They commiserate with the plight of black slaves, Native Americans, and new immigrants who had to fight for freedom despite the rights promised by the U.S. Constitution. Now they are about to learn how the First Amendment to the Bill of Rights guarantees that every American will continue to live in freedom.

Teachers introduce the new unit by asking students to discuss what is meant by freedom of speech, religion, and press. They record responses to these questions on chart paper that is posted in the class. Over the course of two weeks students scour the news media for current events depicting one of these freedoms being challenged. Students also begin generating a list of questions about the First Amendment that can be used to reinforce the essential question: "How does the First Amendment protect our freedom?"

The library media specialist works with the teachers to design a performance task that uses the information search process to guide the inquiry. The following assignment is made:

Grade 8 Assignment

We will be holding a constitutional convention in which we will be defending one of the freedoms guaranteed by the First Amendment and explaining why we need to be vigilant in order to protect it. We will make speeches to the delegation in which we address a current situation that challenges one of the freedoms protected by the First Amendment. In our presentations we should include some historical background and explain how the freedom affects our own lives and the larger society in which we live. Finally, we should suggest what can and should be done to protect the freedoms guaranteed by the Constitution.

The task involves students in an inquiry process that begins with selecting a topic, generating questions, and gathering information from a variety

Figure 3.4
Rubric for note taking

Criteria My notes should be	Advanced	Proficient	Basic
Accurate and complete	All information is accurate. Notes include historical facts and ideas related to freedom. Notes have enough details to support main ideas. Information comes from reliable sources.	All information is accurate. Notes include some historical facts (names, dates, places, etc.) Sources are given.	Some facts are not accurate. No examples from history are given. Sources are not given.
Related to my topic and research questions	All notes are about freedom and the First Amendment. The notes answer all the research questions.	The notes are about freedom. The notes answer most of the research questions.	It is not clear how the notes relate to freedom. The notes answer few of the research questions.
Meaningful to me	All notes are in my own words. I know the meaning of every word I used.	Some notes are copied. There are a few words that I don't understand.	All notes are directly from resources. My notes don't make sense to me.
Well organized	All the notes that answer a question are grouped together. I used bullets to separate notes on a card.	Notes are grouped by the question they answer. It's hard to tell where one note ends and the other begins.	There is no organization to my notes. My notes are a list of facts about freedom.

of resources. Through observation three things become apparent to the instructors:

• Students were quite proficient at accessing information in both print and electronic resources.

- The information being gathered is general in nature and does little to address the specific research questions.
- Students do not know how to extract information that might be critical to their research questions.

The library media specialist identifies note taking as a skill that needs to be developed and offers to take the lead in teaching this part of the process. Following the procedures outlined earlier in Figure 3.3 she involves students in designing a rubric for the note-taking process. Figure 3.4 displays the rubric that both instructors and students created for this unit.

RATING SCALES

What Is a Rating Scale?

A rating scale is similar to a rubric in that it identifies the criteria for successful performance. The critical difference is that the rating scale does not describe varying levels of achievement. Instead, it provides a scale ranging from the highest to the lowest performance levels.

When Might We Use a Rating Scale?

A rating scale is used when the task involves multiple performance targets that need to be assessed. It is used to focus the assessment on specified targets thereby eliminating some of the subjectivity associated with observation of complex tasks. The rating scale is used effectively in situations where performance can be placed along a continuum ranging from the lowest to the highest level of achievement.

Rating scales can be numerical or qualitative. A *numerical scale* uses numbers or assigns points to a continuum of performance levels. The number of scale points can vary. A *qualitative scale* uses adjectives rather than numbers to characterize student performance and label student performance (Herman, Aschbacker, and Winters 1992).

How Do We Construct a Rating Scale?

The first step in constructing any assessment tool is to identify the instructional targets. We approach the construction of the rating scale in much the same way that we develop the rubric—by discussing the components of good work. This discussion leads to the identification of criteria that needs to be assessed. In Figure 3.5 we look at four instructional targets identified for the Bill of Rights project and consider what might be accepted as evidence that the goals have been met.

Figure 3.5
Evidence to assess instructional targets for Bill of Rights unit

Instructional Target	Evidence of Learning
Knowledge/understanding	Shows knowledge of the Bill of Rights. Demonstrates understanding of the rights protected by the First Amendment. Explains the concept of freedom and how it affects his/her own life.
Thinking	Interprets historical events in relation to the First Amendment. Connects current events with history. Expresses a personal point of view about the importance of freedom.
Inquiry and independent learning skills	Poses questions to focus research. Accesses and evaluates information sources. Collects and organizes information. Prepares and presents findings. Assesses process and product.
Presentation	Includes both facts and ideas. Uses facts and information to support a point of view. States what should be done to protect freedom. Speaks clearly and effectively.

How Do We Use a Rating Scale to Assess for Information Literacy?

We continue with the Grade 8 scenario to show how a rating scale might be incorporated into this unit. As they observed students at work on the project, teachers saw the need for a tool to focus their observation and record their general assessment of the key targets. Guided by the rating scale displayed in Figure 3.6, they used the strategies of observation, personal communication, and examination of work samples to rate performance along a continuum. At different points in the project, they compared ratings and planned intervention strategies.

CONCLUSION

The tools described in this chapter are critical front-end instruments that require instructors and students to define criteria for assessment. Precise criteria make it possible to give meaningful feedback, not just

Figure 3.6
Rating scale for assessing targeted aspects of the research process

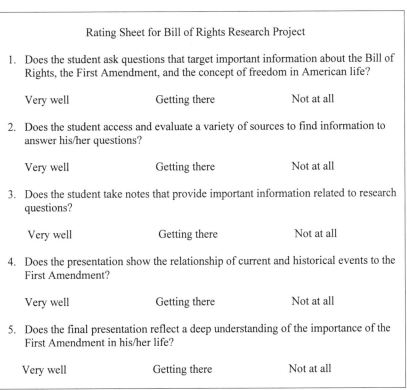

Rating Sheet for Bill of Rights Research Project

1. Does the student ask questions that target important information about the Bill of Rights, the First Amendment, and the concept of freedom in American life?

   Very well   Getting there   Not at all

2. Does the student access and evaluate a variety of sources to find information to answer his/her questions?

   Very well   Getting there   Not at all

3. Does the student take notes that provide important information related to research questions?

   Very well   Getting there   Not at all

4. Does the presentation show the relationship of current and historical events to the First Amendment?

   Very well   Getting there   Not at all

5. Does the final presentation reflect a deep understanding of the importance of the First Amendment in his/her life?

   Very well   Getting there   Not at all

"I like it" or "This is well done" but *why* and *how*. They allow instructors to identify deficiencies in a timely manner. At the same time, students can immediately see what is expected for an assignment (Strickland and Strickland 2000). Involving students in creating and using these tools strengthens their confidence in analyzing their own work (Harada and Yoshina 1997). Such assessment empowers everyone involved in the learning process.

REFERENCES

American Association of School Librarians, and Association for Educational Communications and Technology. 1998. *Information Power: Building Partnerships for Learning.* Chicago, Ill.: American Library Association.

Andrade, Heidi G. 2000. "Using Rubrics to Promote Thinking and Learning," *Educational Leadership* 57, no. 5 (February): 13–18. URL: http://www.ascd.org/readingroom/edlead/0002/Andrade.html (accessed March 23, 2004).

Callison, Daniel. 2003. *Key Words, Concepts and Methods for Information Age Instruction: A Guide to Teaching Information Inquiry.* Baltimore, Md.: LMS Associates.

Donham, Jean. 1998. *Assessment of Information Processes and Products.* McHenry, Ill.: Follett Software Company.

Harada, Violet H., and Joan Yoshina. 1997. "Improving Information Search Process Instruction and Assessment Through Collaborative Action Research," *School Libraries Worldwide* 3, no. 2 (July): 41–55.

Herman, Joan L., Pamela R. Aschbacker, and Lynn Winters. 1992. *A Practical Guide to Alternative Assessment.* Alexandria, Va.: Association for Supervision and Curriculum Development.

Stiggins, Richard. 1997. *Student-Centered Classroom Assessment.* Columbus, Ohio: Prentice Hall.

Strickland, Kathleen, and James Strickland. 2000. *Making Assessment Elementary.* Portsmouth, N.H.: Heinemann.

Todd, Ross J. 2003. "School Libraries Evidence: Seize the Day, Begin the Future," *Library Media Connection* 22, no. 1 (August/September): 12–17.

CHAPTER 4

Tools for Assessments: Conferences, Logs, and Personal Correspondence

In this chapter, we look more closely at assessment tools that invite interaction and communication. The tools highlighted are conferences, logs, and personal communication. As in Chapter 3, discussions are organized around the following key questions:

- What is it?
- When might we use this tool?
- How might we construct this tool?
- How might we use it to assess for information literacy?

CONFERENCES

What Is a Conference?

An assessment conference is any conversation between instructors and students for the purpose of gathering information related to important aspects of a particular learning situation. According to Stiggins (1997) the most natural way to gather achievement data is to talk to the students. The communication may take the form of a casual conversation, a simple question to check for understanding, or a formal interview with specific goals.

When Might We Use Conferences to Assess Learning?

Conferences, which may be formal or informal, take place throughout the day whenever there is a need for information related to learning. Informal conferences occur when the instructor asks a question or engages the student in an on-the-spot conversation to clarify thinking or check for understanding. The instructor often gathers needed information by asking questions like:

- Why did you select this resource? Are there any other resources that might be helpful?
- What keywords did you use? Can you think of other terms to search?

- How can you narrow your topic? What aspects of the topic are most interesting to you?
- What else do you want to find out about the topic?

This kind of natural exchange has a flexibility not associated with more structured assessment strategies. These informal conferences are best used when there is an immediate need for information to guide the learning.

The formal conference, on the other hand, is more like an interview. Formal conferences may be held at specific points in the process so that instructors can monitor progress. For example, conferences held early in the process may focus on topic selection, research questions, or search strategies. Later, students may sign up for conferences to review their notes with the teacher before they work on their presentations. Other conferences are held after the presentation to assess both the process and product. Often the conference schedule is determined in advance and included in each student's action plan.

The library media specialist can play an important role in these conferences. If the goal is for students to become independent users of information, instruction will more than likely follow an information search model. Students will be expected to demonstrate skill in areas like selecting topics and issues; questioning; and accessing, evaluating, organizing, and using information. Scheduling a quick conference early in the process provides an opportunity to identify students who are struggling so that adjustments can be made in a timely manner.

While conferences can be highly effective instructional tools, it is important to note that the formal conference, in particular, is labor intensive. We suggest several ways of managing the task:

- Hold group interviews whenever possible. This works best when students are engaged in team projects.
- Divide up the work. The teacher may briefly confer with students about their topic selection and research questions. The library media specialist may follow up by reviewing search strategies and suggesting additional resources.
- Hold conferences on a selective basis. Use work samples and observations to determine which students need more guidance. Schedule conferences with these students, but insist that every student present evidence of achievement before proceeding.

The time spent talking to students about their research questions, search strategies, and possible resources pay big dividends in terms of the overall success of the project.

How Do We Structure the Conference?

The formal conference, in particular, needs to be planned to ensure success. Consider the following types of questions to guide the planning:

- Which of the instructional targets are best assessed through conferences or interviews?
- What information do we want to gather through the conference?
- What questions will help to elicit the desired information?
- How can we use the interview to guide the student through the process?

Once the conference targets have been clearly identified, instructors develop a list of questions to guide the interview toward evidence collection. Figure 4.1 includes several instructional targets and related interview questions that might be used to shape a conference.

How Do We Use Conferences to Assess for Information Literacy?

Conferencing is a potent tool for developing and assessing information literacy. Many of the exchanges that are so natural to the instructional setting provide valuable information about achievement in terms of the information literacy skills. As students work on their projects, teachers and library media specialists often ask questions that focus on elements of the

Figure 4.1
Linking conferencing questions with instructional targets

Instructional Targets	Interview Questions
Knowledge and understanding	What is the most important thing you learned about your topic? How does this relate to your own life?
Research questions	What else would you like to find out about your topic? Which questions will lead to a deeper understanding of the issues?
Notes	How do these notes help answer your research question? Can you think of any examples to make this point clear?
Product	Who will be your audience? How can you best share your knowledge with them?

research process or product. Those casual conversations that go beyond a simple "How are you doing?" often provide valuable insight into how students are approaching the task. Picture the following scenario:

Grade 6 Scenario

Sixth graders are exploring the theme of civilization. They wrestle with the following overarching questions:

- How can we identify an ancient civilization?
- What aspects of this civilization are still alive in our world today?

Students work in teams to investigate the origin of specific civilizations, summarize their defining features, and identify aspects of these civilizations that still influence our lives today. They use an inquiry process that involves posing questions to drive the research, identifying appropriate resources, reading and evaluating information, taking notes, and creating a product or performance. As a final presentation, all of the sixth-grade classes work on a museum of ancient history where they display their products, give performances, and hold competitions (e.g., the Olympics). The entire school community is invited to participate in the activities.

Throughout the project, a class matrix keeps students focused on the essential questions surrounding the characteristics of civilized societies. Students use the matrix to record their findings and to make generalizations about the civilizations being investigated by various search teams.

For the project described in the scenario, conferencing was included in the plan from the beginning. Students were instructed at the outset to conference with either the teacher or the library media specialist before they began working on their final presentations. They were asked to bring to the conference their research questions, notes, and ideas about how best to share their findings. These items became the focus for the final conference.

Throughout the project, the instructors regularly engaged students in conversation as they worked on the process and the product. In the following example, the library media specialist and a student are discussing the merits of using the Internet to find information about pyramids:

Excerpt from a conference:

LMS: "Who was the author of this web page?"
Student: "It was part of a class project so I guess it was done by a student."
LMS: "Do you think it's a reliable source?"

> *Student:* "I don't know. Maybe I can check out her sources. Some of them are on the Internet so they should be easy to find."
>
> *LMS:* "Where else could you look for information comparing Egyptian pyramids with those built in the New World?"
>
> *Student:* "Well, the Internet is really a great resource, but I guess I could check out some of the books the library has on ancient Egypt."

Informal exchanges like this one helped students to think about the task in different ways. In this situation the library media specialist prodded the student to think more critically about information found on the Internet. Other similar conversations provided guidance and directions as students worked on the different phases of the information search process.

As data were acquired through various assessment strategies, the instructors began to identify students in need of more guidance and support. For these students more structured conferences were scheduled to pinpoint problems and provide necessary direction. The classroom teacher usually initiated these conferences. However, in many instances the library media specialist was asked to follow up when students needed help with search strategies, alternative resources, or other areas specific to the information search process.

LOGS

What Is a Log?

The log is a valuable tool for self-assessment and reflection that can be used by students to monitor their own learning. Students use logs to reflect on what they are learning, how they are learning, and how they feel about the process. Keeping logs encourages students to express their feelings, to reflect on different aspects of the topic, to articulate problems they are having, and to put out a call for help.

Logs have many uses in a classroom and library media center. Students can use them to clarify questions, identify themes, summarize ideas, review discussions, plan future applications, and pose solutions to problems. They are especially powerful tools if students have opportunities to share them with peers and interact through this medium. Importantly, instructors can use them to assess the effectiveness of their teaching and identify valuable clues to student needs and insights (Harada 2002). They allow instructors to get inside the minds of all students and not just those who are highly verbal.

The key to using logs as an assessment tool lies with the prompt. It is critical to design prompts that target specific goals. If, for example, one of the objectives is for students to pursue information that satisfies their own personal interests, the prompt might be: "What aspects of the general topic are you most interested in? How does this topic relate to your own life?"

When Might We Use Logs as Assessment Tools?

We rely on logs to assess many components of information literacy including appreciation of literature, independent learning, and social responsibility. Figure 4.2 provides examples of prompts that might address specific information literacy standards (AASL and AECT 1998).

Figure 4.2
Matching journal prompts with information literacy goals

Information Literacy Goals	Journal Prompts
Accesses information efficiently and effectively.	How did you go about finding the information to answer your research questions? Describe your search strategy.
Evaluates information critically and competently.	Which sources did you find most helpful? What criteria did you use in selecting your sources?
Uses information accurately and creatively.	How will you present your information? Who will your audience be? What main ideas do you want to express? What facts and information will you include in the presentation?
Pursues information related to personal interests.	How does this topic relate to your life? What aspects of the topic are most interesting to you?
Appreciates literature and other creative expressions of information.	What is the best book you read this month (quarter, semester, or year)? How did the book relate to your own life? How does it compare with other books that you have read?
Recognizes the importance of information to a democratic society.	What information will you need in order to make a good decision? How can this information be used to solve problems in our community?
Participates effectively in groups to pursue and generate information.	What can you contribute to the project? What special skills or knowledge do you bring to the group effort? How do you feel about working in this group?

The value of logging is not limited to the information search process. This strategy can be used to assess feelings and attitudes as well as skills and knowledge. When students are asked to respond honestly to a piece of literature by telling how it relates to their own lives, they are encouraged to think more deeply and to make connections they may have overlooked during the initial reading. The resulting entry may provide teachers and library media specialists with a valuable window into the student's thoughts and feelings.

As an example, after fifth graders read the opening chapters of *The Island of the Blue Dolphins*, they were given the following prompts: "Have you ever felt alone or abandoned? How do you think Karana felt when the ship left without her and her brother? What do you think will happen to them?" Note the empathy expressed in the following student response:

Example of a student log:

Karana must have really felt abandoned. Her father was killed, and now the boat left with everyone on board but her brother and her. They were all alone on the island except for the wild dogs. She must have been scared stiff, but she had to act brave for her brother's sake. She is very strong on the inside.

I don't think I could have been so tough. What would I do if something happened to my parents and I was left in charge? I wouldn't know how to find food for my sisters and me. And even though I like dogs, I wouldn't know how to protect my sisters from the wild ones that lived on the island.

I think the boat will come back to get them, or maybe they will send a rescue team. Karana can send up smoke signals to let them know where they are. But in the meantime, they will have to live by eating plants and berries and stuff like that. If I were Karana, I would feel very lonely and scared. I hope someone comes for them soon.

Log keeping is often used in conjunction with other assessment methods. For example, after students have worked on creating a rubric, we might ask them to respond to a question like "Which criteria do you think are most important for a successful project? Why do you think this?" After a conference, we might ask students to reflect on what happened at the conference and if it was helpful. Whether we use it alone to assess students' reactions to a literary experience or as a tool for reflection during a complex project, the journal is an invaluable component of the assessment toolbox.

How Do We Facilitate the Use of Logs?

The log may be structured to assess learning targets over time. When this is the intent, students respond to a few prompts on a regular basis so that progress can be measured throughout the process. Figure 4.3 is an example of a log developed to help primary students reflect on their progress as independent learners.

Logs may take many other forms depending on the intended learning goals (S.C.O.R.E. Language Arts n.d.). Here are several examples. Figure 4.4 is an example of a log that requires students to summarize their various learning activities in a project and consider application of that learning.

Figure 4.5 is an example of a log that invites students to share affective as well as cognitive responses.

Figure 4.6 is an example of a log that encourages student response to a literary piece.

Figure 4.3
Learning log for primary research projects

My Research Log

Today I worked on _____

I learned that _____

Here are some problems that I had _____

Tomorrow I am going to _____

This is how I feel about myself as a researcher: (Write your name by the one that is you.)

SAD   HAPPY   CONFUSED

Figure 4.4
Example of synthesis log A

What I did
What I learned
How I can use it

Figure 4.5
Example of synthesis log B

What happened?	How do I feel about it?	What did I learn as a result?

Figure 4.6
Example of literary response log

Which of the characters seemed more real to you? Why was this?	
Were you able to make connections between events in the story and your own experiences? How so?	
Were there any striking phrases and images in the story? Why do you think they were chosen? How do they add to the story?	

How Do We Use Logs to Assess for Information Literacy?

Grade 10 Scenario

A high school biology class is investigating the complex relationship between science and ethics. An important goal of the science curriculum is to provide students with a means for understanding how scientific decisions may be influenced by the ethics and values of various groups within the community. With this in mind, biology teachers have designed a unit focusing on recent developments in bioethics. The study is framed by the essential question: "How do values and ethics influence scientific thought?"

Students form search teams to investigate topics like evolution, stem cell research, organ transplants, cloning, and the use of human and animal subjects in scientific experiments. They use various print, electronic, and personal resources to develop an overview of their topics and to identify different points of view related to the issue. The culminating activity is a series of panel discussions focusing on the research topics. Each student on the team expresses the point of view of one of the key parties who might be affected by the scientific research. Class members who are not participating in a particular discussion direct questions at the panel to clarify the issues. Each panel discussion ends with a peer evaluation and a discussion of the values and ethics raised by the team members.

The library media specialist contributes to the process by:

- Helping teachers identify issues for students to investigate.
- Providing short articles to introduce the issues.
- Helping teachers to keep the discussion focused on values and ethics and their impact on scientific decisions.
- Developing mini-lessons on selected phases of the information search process, namely, asking questions to frame the search, identifying potential sources of information, and taking notes to support a particular point of view.

Throughout the unit students use their logs to reflect on what they are learning and how it relates to the essential question. The prompts are carefully chosen to keep students focused on the ethical dimensions of scientific reasoning. For example:

- Why is this research important?
- What arguments are given for and against the research?
- How do you think this research will benefit or harm humanity?

- Who has an interest in supporting or stopping this research? Why?
- Do you think this research might have unintended side effects? What might they be?
- Who should pay for this research? Should it be publicly or privately funded?
- How costly will this research be in terms of both money and unintended consequences? Is the benefit worth the cost?

When the purpose is to assess proficiency in terms of the information literacy standards, the questions may be quite different. Figure 4.7 displays some prompts that are used to gather information needed to assess aspects of information literacy.

Figure 4.7
Prompts for assessing aspects of information literacy

Purpose of Assessment	Example of Prompt
Choice of topic	Which scientific developments have the greatest potential for good? For harm? Which research are you most interested in? Why?
Research questions	What do you already know about your choice of topic? What would you need to find out in order to support it or oppose it?
Selecting and evaluating information sources	What criteria did you use to select resources? Which sources did you find most helpful? Which were of little or no help? Give reasons for your response.
Using information to make a persuasive argument	Whose point of view will you represent on the panel? Will you be supporting or opposing continuation of the research? What reasons will you give for your position? How will you validate your information?
Working as a team to produce and communicate knowledge	Was it helpful to work as a team? Why or why not? What did you contribute to the group effort? What did you learn from the panel discussions that you could not have learned on your own?

This is what one student had to say in response to the question about choice of topic.

Example of a student log:

I think I am most interested in stem cell research. I don't know a lot about it, but the article we read says that scientists are using stem cells to cure diseases like Parkinson's and Alzheimer's. My grandfather is in the early stages of Alzheimer's disease. The doctor said that even if he takes his medicine, there is no cure for this condition. I saw on TV that some people get so sick that they don't even recognize their own children and grandchildren. I hope this doesn't happen to my grandpa.

Stem cell research may help people with other diseases, too. Scientists don't really know yet where the research will lead, but I think a lot of people will be able to live better lives if the government would support stem cell research. On the other hand, if the research doesn't get funded, more and more people will die from incurable diseases.

A reflection like this tells the instructors several things about the writer. Importantly, the student has chosen a topic that is personally meaningful to her. She knows enough about the topic to identify it as an important area for scientific study. She recognizes the value of the research and has some sense of its potential benefits. However, the student does not seem to be aware of the controversy surrounding the topic. The library media specialist suggests that she include a research question focusing on the arguments offered by opponents of stem cell research.

Log keeping is an open-ended process that provides valuable insight into aspects of information literacy that are often difficult to pin down. These include skills and attitudes related to independent learning and social responsibility as well as information literacy. Because collaboration and teamwork were goals of this project, students were asked to express their feelings about the group experience by responding to the following questions:

- How did you feel about working with a team on this project?
- How would you rate your contributions to the group?
- Do you think the panel discussion was an effective way of dealing with issues of values and ethics in science?
- What contributed to the success or failure of the project?

The student who selected stem cell research as her project wrote this in her response.

Example of a student log:

Being part of a panel discussion was a good experience for me. Because we all represented different parties in the dispute, I got to see how stem cell research was viewed by doctors, patients, and religious groups. I found out that the cost of the research was very high so it was important to convince politicians that it was important.

One of the first things my group did was to decide who would represent which point of view on the panel. I said I wanted to speak for the families of people with Alzheimer's. Other kids took the parts of a patient, a doctor, a taxpayer, and a senator whose committee decided which health-related projects to fund.

Everyone agreed that we needed to begin the research by finding out what the pros and cons were for experimenting with stem cells. We also wanted to get information about the other diseases that might be cured through stem cell research; and our teacher said that we should learn more about how stem cells work. After we wrote our questions, we made a list of all the resources we could use. Then we divided up the work.

My job was to interview family members to find out how they were affected by the disease. I put their comments on a T-chart to show the pros and cons of supporting the research. This information is different from what other people found by looking on the Internet and reading magazine articles. Having different kinds of information made the panel discussion more interesting.

Even though we worked well together, we didn't always agree about things like funding and whether the benefits were worth the cost. So there were some arguments, and sometimes we challenged each other to prove a point. The disagreements turned out to be good practice for the panel discussion. The best thing about my group was that we all learned from each other. That's a good thing.

This reflection clearly indicates that the student sees the benefits of collaboration and understands her role on the team. Log entries from various students gave instructors a better understanding of the role of group dynamics in student projects. In general the logs showed that

- Students prefer working in groups to working independently.
- Some structure is needed for groups to work effectively.
- Groups work best when each student understands his or her role and responsibilities.
- Instructors need to facilitate and guide the group interaction toward the stated objectives.

Before leaving the topic of learning logs, it is critical to emphasize the importance of using logs in conjunction with other assessment tools. While logs provide valuable insight into student achievement, more quantifiable methods are needed to complete the assessment picture. In the bioethics unit, for example, several assessment tools were used in addition to the learning logs. These included a checklist to monitor the steps in the information search process and a rubric for assessing questioning and note-taking skills.

PERSONAL CORRESPONDENCE

What Is Personal Correspondence?

Davies and her colleagues (1992) have written extensively about the power of personal correspondence as an assessment tool. Personal correspondence includes letters and notes written by students that focus on specific learning goals and provide information important to the learning process. Letters and notes have the added advantage of a real audience from whom feedback may be expected.

When Might We Use Personal Correspondence to Assess Learning?

Letters of invitation, appreciation, and explanation are a natural way for students to involve others in the learning process. Children write letters to their parents in which they point out important aspects of a project or summarize key discoveries. A note to the teacher might solicit feedback about specific aspects of a student's work. Similarly, students can exchange notes that provide informative feedback and serve as a vehicle for peer review. Figure 4.8 presents several instructional targets for which letters and notes may be used appropriately as an assessment tool.

How Do We Construct the Correspondence?

If the purpose of the correspondence is to assess some aspect of learning, the initial instruction needs to provide a structure for students to follow. For older students this can be accomplished by discussing sample notes and pointing out how key elements are addressed. However, more direction may be needed to achieve the desired outcomes for younger learners. Figure 4.9 represents a template we developed for upper elementary students to write personal invitations to the school's annual science fair. Notice that the student is asked to mention three things that he considers most important to his project.

Figure 4.8
Using letters and notes to assess instructional goals

Instructional goal	Correspondence
Students will select and read books that satisfy their personal interests.	Students write notes to their parents telling about the books they are reading. They include details explaining why the book is interesting to them.
Students will use the information search process to create personal knowledge.	Students write letters to the editor explaining their personal viewpoint on an issue and giving reasons for their stand.
Students will participate effectively in groups to pursue and generate information.	Students write notes to their peers in which they make positive comments about a product or performance.
Students will strive for excellence in information searching and knowledge generation.	Students write notes to their teachers expressing their feelings about the search process and seeking help with specific problems.

Figure 4.9
Template for invitation to a science fair

May 10, 2005

Dear Mom and Dad,

Please come to our science fair. It will be held in the school library from May 15 to

May 19. The title of my project is _____

In my project I wanted to _____

Three things I would like to point out about my project are:

_____

_____

_____

Your son or daughter,

_____

Figure 4.10
Template for parents' response

```
                                                              May 15, 2005

Dear _____,

        Thank you for sharing your project with us. It showed us that you have learned

_____.

We especially liked _____

One question we have is _____

Love,


_____

```

The template displayed in Figure 4.10 is provided for parents to comment on the project.

How Do We Use Personal Correspondence to Assess for Information Literacy?

Grade 7 Scenario

A seventh-grade health class is engaged in a problem-based unit on wellness. Students have used the Internet to search for health-related problems of particular interest to adolescents. One group has decided to focus on the problem of obesity. Their task will be to research the causes and effects of the problem, to find out what can be done to counteract the problem, and to initiate a public relations campaign to educate the community about the dangers of the problem. Students use an information search model to guide them through the process of asking questions; accessing resources; collecting, evaluating, and organizing information; and planning an effective presentation.

In Figure 4.11 we take a look at some of the notes and letters produced during the wellness unit.

Figure 4.11
Notes and letters used to assess the information literacy process

Description of the Correspondence	Writing Sample
A note to teachers explaining the choice of topic and some of the questions they have about it	*Dear Mrs. Brown,* *Our group decided to research obesity because we found out that one out of every five kids is seriously overweight and that this condition leads to many other health problems like diabetes, heart problems, and some kinds of cancer.* *Some questions we want to answer are:* • *How do you know if you are obese?* • *What are the causes of obesity?* • *How can obesity be cured or controlled?*
A note written to provide informative feedback on the products and performances of other students	*Dear Emily, Jon, and Ethan,* *I really like your video about the importance of exercise. The part I liked best was when you showed the kinds of exercises kids can do to stay fit.* *One thing I didn't understand was why some people exercised but didn't lose weight. Can you explain that?*
A note to parents explaining the final product and what was learned through the process	*Dear Mom and Dad,* *I hope you will read the brochure my group made about obesity. We wanted to tell kids and their parents about the causes and effects of obesity and to show what can be done about it. We found most of the information on the Internet and by talking to people from the Department of Health. We collected some of the information by having kids keep a record of what they ate and then we made a graph to show the results. We also made a survey to find out how often kids exercised.* *We found out that the main causes of obesity are a poor diet and lack of regular exercise. We think the way to solve the problem is through education. That's why we made the brochure.*

CONCLUSION

Conferences, logs, letters, and notes add another dimension to the assessment picture provided by the more structured strategies described in Chapter 3. The open-ended nature of these assessment methods creates a window into students' thoughts and feelings that might otherwise remain closed to inspection. They allow instructors to see not only what a student knows, but also how he or she has come to acquire the knowledge. These methods cast a light on aspects of learning that are difficult to measure using criterion-based assessments.

As students talk and write about what they are learning, they become more engaged in the process. Honest reflection leads to deeper levels of understanding about both the learning process and the student as a learner. Prompts and questions that are meaningful and purposeful can be the catalyst for change and growth (Martin-Kniep 2000). Students who are engaged in talking and writing about what they are thinking and how they are learning are well on their way to a lifetime of learning.

REFERENCES

American Association of School Librarians, and Association for Educational Communications and Technology. 1998. *Information Power: Building Partnerships for Learning*. Chicago, Ill.: American Library Association.

Davies, Anne, Caren Cameron, Colleen Politano, and Katheen Gregory. 1992. *Together Is Better: Collaborative Assessment, Evaluation and Reporting*. Winnipeg, Canada: Peguis Publishers.

Harada, Violet H. 2002. "Personalizing the Information Search Process: A Case Study of Journal Writing with Elementary-Age Students," *School Library Media Research*. URL: http://www.ala.org/ala/aasl/aaslpubsandjournals/slmrb/slmrcontents/volume52002/harada.htm (accessed February 11, 2004).

Martin-Kniep, Giselle. 2000. "Reflection: A Key to Developing Greater Self-Understanding." In *Becoming a Better Teacher: Eight Innovations That Work*. Alexandria, Va.: Association for Supervision and Curriculum Development. URL: http://www.ascd.org/publications/books/2000martinkniep/chapter7.html (accessed February 11, 2004).

S.C.O.R.E. Language Arts. n.d. *Schools of California Online Resources in Education: Journals*. URL: http://www.sdcoe.k12.ca.us/score/actbank/tjournal.htm (accessed February 11, 2004).

Stiggins, Richard J. 1997. *Student-Centered Classroom Assessment*. Columbus, Ohio: Prentice Hall, Inc.

CHAPTER 5

Tools for Assessment: Graphic Organizers

In this chapter, we examine several types of graphic organizers that are frequently used in schools. These include concept maps, webs, K-W-L charts, and matrices. The discussion for each tool is organized around the following key questions:

- What is it?
- When might we use the tool?
- How do we construct this tool?
- How do we use it to assess for information literacy?

WHAT ARE GRAPHIC ORGANIZERS?

Graphic organizers are visual representations of thinking. They contribute to learning by providing a structure that supports critical thinking and problem solving. Callison (2003) defines organizers as

tools or techniques that provide identification and classification along with possible relationships or connections among ideas, concepts, and issues. Organizers are useful to the learner when given in advance of instruction and often serve as clues to ideas that the instructor plans to introduce. (251)

Organizers are not a new concept. David Ausubel's (1967) research with advance organizers in the 1960s has provided the foundation for effective teaching based on visual mapping of concepts and ideas. According to Pappas (1997), a range of organizers have been used in various disciplines. As she explains:

The math discipline uses Venn diagrams to examine numerical relationships. Flow charts are used to illustrate a decision-making process in math and computer science. The language arts teachers have been using webs to explore relationships of characters and plot in fiction stories. (30)

Graphic organizers can be designed for specific learning objectives (Ekhaml 1998) including:

- Seeing connections and patterns
- Outlining ideas

- Comparing and contrasting ideas
- Showing cause and effect
- Developing a global view of a topic or an issue
- Preparing summaries and conclusions
- Facilitating the retention of key ideas
- Recalling or retelling of literature
- Organizing the research process

Organizers must be broad and conceptual in nature so that they "provide a large umbrella under which many more specific items can be identified, discussed, and related" (Callison 2003, 252). Figure 5.1 provides examples of organizers that might be devised for different learning objectives.

The same organizer that is used as an instructional tool can be used to assess various aspects of information literacy. In this chapter we present four basic graphic organizers—concept maps, webs, K-W-L charts, and matrices—that are well suited for use in assessing a range of information literacy skills.

CONCEPT MAPS

What Is a Concept Map?

A concept map is a visual diagram that is used to show the links among important related concepts. The technique of concept mapping as a tool for learning originated with Joseph Novak (qtd. in *Concept Mapping* n.d.) of Cornell University who believed that the process helped students to integrate new information with prior knowledge. Concept maps use a hierarchical structure to show the relative importance of ideas. The process involves identifying important concepts, creating spaces and labels for each concept, and constructing links to show relationships (Willson n.d.). It helps learners clarify what they have read or heard. It affords a visual sketch of key terms around a central idea or concept (Callison 2003).

When Might We Use a Concept Map?

Meaningful learning involves the assimilation of new concepts and propositions into existing cognitive structures. Simply put, concept mapping provides a structure for organizing existing knowledge and connecting newly acquired ideas to it. According to Callison (2003) "because the process involves choices and a focus, along with some organization of terms, the learner becomes engaged with the content" (139). Concept maps might be used to:

- Organize a unit of study around major concepts
- Show the relative importance of ideas

Figure 5.1
Examples of organizers for different learning objectives

Learning Objectives	Graphic Organizers	Examples
To explore aspects of the topic or theme	Idea web	
To compare and contrast	Compare/contrast matrix	
To show cause and effect	Fishbone map	
To provide a framework for solving problems	Problem solving model	
To categorize or show relationships of parts to whole	Tree map	
To connect new learning to prior knowledge	K-W-L chart	
To plan a multimedia presentation or a web page	Storyboard	

- Promote deeper levels of understanding
- Increase retention of important concepts
- Assess convergent thinking and problem solving
- Recognize patterns and relationships

How Do We Construct a Concept Map?

The design of a concept map should reflect the relationships among the ideas being represented. Because concept maps are created for different purposes, no two are exactly alike. The final design of the map is determined by factors like:

- Instructional goals underlying the construction of the map
- Complexity of the ideas being studied
- Intrinsic structure of the area of knowledge being represented
- Ability of students to identify major concepts and to show how they relate

Figure 5.2 outlines key steps involved in creating a concept map for instruction and assessment purposes.

How Do We Use a Concept Map to Assess for Information Literacy?

Grade 3 Scenario
   A third-grade class is learning about the rain forest. Three essential questions are used to focus learning around important concepts:

- How are the plants and animals in the rain forest dependent on each other?
- How has human activity affected the plants and animals that live in the rainforest?
- Why is it important to protect the rain forest?

Each student will be responsible for:

- Researching one of the rain forest plants or animals
- Creating a visual representation of the plant or animal
- Preparing a sign identifying the plant or animal and providing important information relevant to the research questions
- Making a poster to promote actions that will save the rain forest

Students will work in teams to create a simulated rain forest environment in the classroom. The design will start with the four layers of life and include visuals representing the plants and animals that live in each zone. Students will post signs with important information about the different organisms. As guests walk through the rain forest, they will hear ambient sounds created with musical instruments. The third graders will serve as guides and explain the exhibit to parents. They will also help the younger students with reading and interpretation.

Figure 5.2
Steps in constructing a concept map

Step in the Process	Questions to Guide the Process
1. Clarify instructional targets.	What are your instructional goals? What do you want your students to know and be able to do?
2. Identify the most important concepts.	What are the most important ideas you want students to take from the study? How will you involve students in identifying important concepts?
3. Tap into students' prior knowledge.	What do students know about the topic? How do they know this? Which of these ideas is most important?
4. Design a graph that shows relationships among major concepts.	How can students graphically represent the major concept? How can they show related concepts?
5. Create links to connect concepts.	How are these concepts connected? What is the relationship between major and subordinate concepts?
6. Provide a system for expanding the map.	How can students add new information to the map? How will they differentiate between new and prior knowledge?
7. Use the map for assessment.	What information did students have at the beginning of the study? Was it accurate? What did they add during the study? How is it connected to what they already knew?

Figure 5.3
Concept map for the rain forest ecosystem

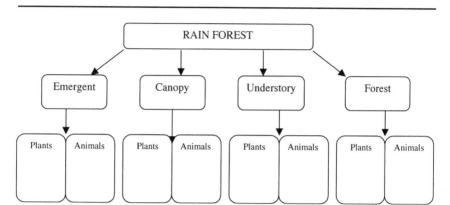

The primary goal for this unit was to develop an understanding of the rain forest as a system of interconnected parts. To reinforce this concept the instructors worked with students to create a concept map. That map, illustrated in Figure 5.3, shows the complex relationships that exist in the rain forest ecosystem.

The study of the rain forest began with a visit to *Zoom Rainforests* (Enchanted Learning.com 2004). Here students found out that the rain forest is a living environment that is a haven for millions of different plants and animals. They examined a visual representation of the rain forest that clearly illustrated and labeled the four vegetative zones. They learned about human activities that impact the health of the rain forest. Finally, they used the web site to find the names of plants and animals that lived in each of the layers. These names were added to the concept map and used as a point of reference throughout the unit study.

The map provided a framework for the research. Students were divided into teams representing the four layers of life. Each student in the group chose one of the plants or animals as a research topic. They used a variety of print and nonprint resources to collect information that was accurate and relevant in terms of the essential questions for the unit.

Throughout the process teachers asked questions like the following to help students understand the rain forest as a system of interdependent organisms:

- Why do the animals live in different parts of the rain forest? What conditions make some prefer the forest floor, some the understory, and still others the canopy?
- Why do so many plants and animals live in the rain forest?

- How do rain forest animals depend on each other? How do they depend on the plants?
- What are the dangers facing the rain forest? How does the fate of one organism affect others in the ecosystem?

Following a model developed by Inspiration.com (n.d.), the instructors helped students design their own organizers with spaces for the topic, questions, and notes. They used arrows to show the relationship between the cells on the map. One student's map is illustrated in Figure 5.4.

The library media specialist used students' concept maps to assess important aspects of the information literacy process, including the ability to:

- Access information from more than one resource
- Take notes using key words
- Show how one concept relates to another
- Organize information in a logical manner

Students added their notes including their sources of information to the class concept map on the bulletin board. The map served as a blueprint for the research on the rain forest environment.

Figure 5.4
Concept map for howler monkey

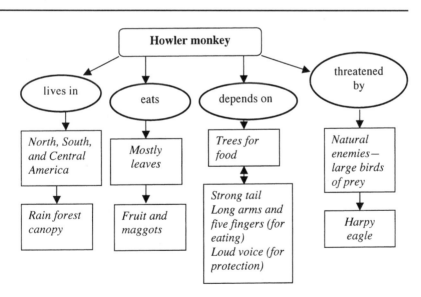

Write here where you found your information:

I found my information on the Enchanted Learning site and in the book Howler Monkeys (Animals of the Rain Forest) by Sandra Donovan

WEBS

What Is a Web?

A web is a graphic organizer that clusters key words around a central topic or main idea. It provides a structure that allows students to show how facts and ideas are related to each other and to the main topic. Webs give students a flexible framework for organizing and prioritizing information (Inspiration Software n.d.). Students select a topic, a theme, a question, or even a piece of literature and expand the concept by brainstorming attributes, examples, questions, or subtopics that relate to it.

When Might We Use a Web?

The web is an effective means of assessing divergent thinking. It provides a graphic representation of internal thought processes and gives students a framework that encourages adventurous thinking. Vandergrift (1994) indicates that webbing allows for ideas to be expressed and captured without the constraints of an ordered progression. Because it is characterized by a free flow of thinking, webbing is an effective strategy for:

- Generating ideas and questions
- Brainstorming prior knowledge about the topic
- Expanding thinking about the topic
- Displaying the range of subtopics related to a theme or topic

Webbing is also an effective way to engage students in the appreciation and interpretation of literature. This type of web is easily created by writing the name of a literary piece in the center of the paper and brainstorming related ideas around it. These ideas may include:

- Narrative elements—setting, characters, plot, theme, resolution
- Related pieces of literature—books or poems with a similar theme
- Research topics suggested by the literature
- Other works by the author

Teachers and library media specialists have found webbing to be an effective way to facilitate small group work. When students cooperate to construct a web, they incorporate the ideas and contributions of each member of the group (Inspiration Software n.d.). As an added bonus, students can use their webs to focus on different aspects of a collaborative research project.

How Do We Construct a Web?

Webbing is a dynamic process. It begins with a question, a theme, or an issue and grows to reflect a wide range of thinking about the concept. To construct a web we apply the following procedure.

- Write the main topic or driving question in the middle of the paper and draw a circle around it.
- Brainstorm ideas related to the topic or question.
- Group similar ideas from the list.
- Label each group.
- Draw small circles around the main one. Make one circle for each group and write the label inside.
- Draw lines to connect the small circles with the main one.
- Extend the web as you discover new information or develop fresh insights.

How Do We Use a Web to Assess for Information Literacy?

> *Grade 5 Scenario*
> The fifth grade is planning a colonial fair. They will be preparing booths, exhibits, and activities to simulate life in colonial times. Two essential questions will provide a focus for the event:
>
> - How did the colonists live?
> - How did individuals contribute to the welfare of the colony?
>
> Students are divided into two teams with each group addressing one of the overarching questions. Group meetings are held to plan the research and the presentation. During these sessions students work collaboratively to:
>
> - Outline the information to be presented
> - Brainstorm how to present information
> - Decide *who* will be responsible for *what*

The group addressing the question "How did the colonists live?" began by creating a web with the question at the center. Their web is illustrated in Figure 5.5.

The group responsible for addressing the question "How did individuals contribute to the welfare of the colony?" decided to focus on the trades and to show how they contributed to colonial life. Their web is illustrated in Figure 5.6.

Figure 5.5
Web for "How did the colonists live?"

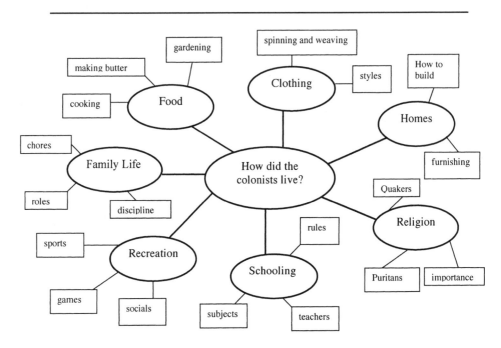

Figure 5.6
Web showing contributions made by colonial tradespeople

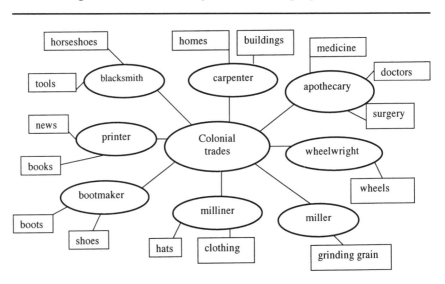

Each group used the web as a basis for topic selection. Students worked in interest groups of two or three to select a subtopic, draft research questions, and plan their presentations for the colonial fair. The web served as a conceptual framework allowing students to see how their research and presentation fit into the bigger picture. For the library media specialist the web was a way to see at a glance how students were approaching their research in terms of the essential questions.

The colonial fair was an event to remember. Students dressed in breeches, vests, aprons, and caps and treated their peers to Johnny Cakes and homemade butter. They attended a Puritan church service and learned to read with a hornbook. They demonstrated the arts of quilting, weaving, and candle making. They organized foot races and games of hopscotch and hide-and-seek. In improvised workshops they explained the work of carpenters, blacksmiths, and wheelwrights. Visitors to the fair were given colonial currency to purchase goods and services at the apothecary, the print shop, the millinery, and the general store. In the end the children all agreed that the colonists led difficult but busy lives and that every member of the community, including the children, contributed to the colony's success.

K-W-L CHARTS

What Is a K-W-L Chart?

The K-W-L chart, originally created by Donna Ogle (1986) and illustrated by James Bellanca (1992), is a tool commonly used to help students plan and assess their research projects. The chart usually consists of three columns:

K—Students use this column to write what they *know* about the topic.

W—In this column students write what they *want to learn* about the topic.

L—Students write here what they *learned* through their reading and research.

Teachers and library media specialists have adapted the basic structure of the K-W-L chart to serve specific purposes. For example, the North Central Regional Educational Laboratory web site (www.ncrel.org/sdrs/areas/issues/students/learning/lrlkwlh.htm) describes tables that add a fourth column for "How can we learn more?"

When Might We Use a K-W-L Chart?

The K-W-L chart is one of the simplest strategies for organizing students' thinking about a topic or an issue; therefore, it is especially effective in work with younger children. Figure 5.7 describes how the K-W-L chart might be used at different points in the research process.

Figure 5.7
Using the K-W-L chart to organize the research process

Part of the Chart	Purpose
(K) Beginning: Explore the general topic	To activate thinking about what is already known about the topic and to pose questions to guide the search.
(W) Middle: Pose questions Evaluate and collect information	To record new information and insights as they are uncovered.
(L) End: Organize and present information Assess process and product	To reflect on what has been learned through the research, to make connections.

Figure 5.8
Basic K-W-L chart

TOPIC:		
This is what I KNOW	This is what I WONDER	This is what I LEARNED

The K-W-L chart is often used as a group strategy to record the collective thinking of the class about the general topic. It is also used to guide independent learning by providing a structure for students to reflect on prior knowledge, pose questions for further study, and reflect on what has been learned.

How Do We Construct a K-W-L Chart?

The K-W-L chart is a three-column table that provides space for students to record their responses. Figure 5.8 displays a basic K-W-L chart.

When the task involves the information search process, library media specialists may prefer to use a variation known as the K-W-H-L strategy. In this case, the table might look more like the one in Figure 5.9. In this

Figure 5.9
K-W-H-L chart

TOPIC:			
What I KNOW	What I WONDER	HOW I will find out	What I LEARNED

example the *How* column is used to consider possible resources and strategies for finding information.

How Do We Use a K-W-L (or K-W-H-L) Chart to Assess for Information Literacy?

Grade 1 Scenario
   A first-grade class wants to select a pet for the classroom. Students brainstorm criteria to assess the characteristics of an appropriate pet and brainstorm possible pets. In pairs, students select different pets to research. They also have opportunities to interview a veterinarian and take a field trip to a local pet shop. As a class they share their research results and vote for their class pet.

To launch the project described in the above scenario, the teacher posted a large K-W-H-L chart in the front of the classroom where children recorded what they knew about pets and what they wanted to find out. The teacher scheduled time for the class to meet with the library media specialist so that they could discuss their need for information and talk about how and where the information might be found to answer their questions. The library media specialist worked closely with the teacher to help students plan a search strategy. As they developed fresh insights, the children charted what they learned with their teacher's help.

   Throughout the process, group discussions focused on comparing what was known at the outset with what was being learned. Opportunities

Figure 5.10
K-W-H-L chart for pet project

WE KNOW	WE WONDER	HOW WE WILL FIND OUT	WHAT WE LEARNED
Pets live in your house or yard.	What animals make good pets?	Look in books about pets. Ask the vet.	Pets should not be wild animals. Pets shouldn't be too big, or you won't be able to feed them or keep them in the classroom.
Pets are tame. They won't hurt you.	How can you train a pet so it won't hurt anyone?	Look in books under "training." Ask a person who trains pets.	Treat your pet with kindness. Reward your pet for good behavior. Be patient with your pet.
Cats, dogs, fish, and birds make good pets.	How can you tell which animal will be a good pet?	Look in books. Ask people at the Humane Society.	Watch the animal in the pet store or kennel.
You have to feed your pet and clean up after it.	What else do you have to do to take care of your pet?	Ask the person at the pet store or the Humane Society. Look in books about the kind of pet you choose. See if there is a web site about your pet.	Feed it and change the water everyday. If it's a fish, keep the tank clean by putting in snails. If it's a bird, put clean paper in the cage. Dogs and cats need shots.

were provided for students to reflect on the *how* as well as the *what* of learning. Under the skilled direction of the teacher and library media specialist, the K-W-H-L chart provided graphic evidence of learning and self-evaluation. Figure 5.10 represents the final version of the chart.

MATRICES

What Is a Matrix?

A matrix is a grid that can be used to show similarities and differences among items with comparable characteristics (Marzano et al. 2001). The primary purpose of the matrix is to guide thinking by helping students organize their ideas and make meaningful comparisons. Because the matrix presents information in a visual format, it is a valuable tool for helping students to see the "big picture" even as it displays all of the parts. The process of constructing and using a matrix to analyze and synthesize information leads to deeper understanding—the ultimate goal of learning.

When Might We Use a Matrix?

A matrix is used to systematically organize and display information and to compare and contrast topics and subtopics. Often, a class matrix is constructed to model the process and to represent the collective thinking of the group. Once they know how it works, students create their own matrices to:

- Take notes
- Make comparisons
- Form generalizations based on evidence
- Synthesize findings
- Display information in a systematic manner

How Do We Construct a Matrix?

To construct a matrix, students start with three basic questions:

- What items do we want to compare?
- What characteristics can be used to make the comparison?
- How are the items alike? How are they different?

Guided by these questions, students create a grid that places the items being compared on one axis and the characteristics on the other. In the remaining cells they write how the items are alike and how they are different.

Figure 5.11
Model for constructing a comparison matrix

	1st point of comparison	2nd point of comparison	3rd point of comparison
Item A			
Item B			
Item C			
How are the items alike?			
How are the items different?			
Conclusion or generalization			

To construct a comparison matrix, students use a template similar to the one illustrated in Figure 5.11.

How Do We Use a Matrix to Assess for Information Literacy?

Middle School Scenario

Middle school students will be participating in the Kids Voting Program. They will accompany their parents to polling places and use special ballots to cast their votes for important national, state, and local offices. A speaker from the state election office visits the class to explain the process and encourage participation. One student asks, "How do we know who to vote for?" The teacher seizes the opportunity to engage the class in a discussion of issues. Two questions are used to frame the discussion and the subsequent search for information:

- What are the important issues in this election?
- Where do the different candidates stand in respect to these issues?

The library media specialist and the social studies teachers developed a unit plan around these essential questions. Their goals were to encourage thoughtful participation in the voting process and to develop informed voters who made reasoned choices based upon an analysis of the issues. The information search process provided an instructional model steering the learning toward these goals.

The unit began with students scouring the news media for articles dealing with the candidates and the issues. These articles were discussed, analyzed, and debated as the class tried to pin down the important themes. As issues were identified, they were posted on a wall chart to be added to or modified as new information was uncovered.

The library media specialist showed students how to use the Internet to find out which offices were open and who the candidates were for these positions. The class was divided into three groups representing national, state, and local candidates. The first task confronting each group was to determine what the important issues were for their level of government. The instructors helped students design a matrix to compare where the candidates for a particular office stood on each issue. Figure 5.12 was used as a model for the matrices.

Students read campaign literature and, in some cases, attended rallies sponsored by local political organizations. They used e-mail and the telephone to gather additional information on the candidates and the issues. Instruction focused on asking the right questions and keeping an accurate record of the responses. Students honed their interview skills through role-playing and learned how to use the tape recorder and video camera to capture the message.

Teachers and library media specialists used the matrix to track the progress of individuals within the group and to engage students in an ongoing conversation about the issues. The matrix documented students' ability to compare and contrast, to make generalizations, and to reach

Figure 5.12
Matrix for comparing candidates and issues

	Candidate A	Candidate B	Candidate C
Issue 1			
Issue 2			
Issue 3			
Which issues do they agree on?			
Which issues do they disagree on?			
Which overall position do you support? Why?			

conclusions based on evidence. It provided a framework for collaborative learning and kept students focused on the goals of the project. For the library media specialist the matrix was an effective tool for gauging students' ability to gather information using a variety of less traditional sources and techniques, including e-mail, personal interviews, campaign literature, guest speakers, and political debates.

As students learned more about the candidates and their positions, they began to align themselves with particular nominees. Debates were held in which student candidates wrangled over the issues. Campaign slogans were printed on homemade buttons, and students lobbied for their favorite candidates in the classroom, the cafeteria, and the library media center.

The turnout on election day was overwhelming. Students came to the polls armed with information about the candidates. Their enthusiasm and zeal served as a reminder to the entire community that voting is a dynamic process requiring careful study and the active engagement of informed citizens. Eighth graders and their parents agreed that they had learned some valuable lessons about the importance of voting in a democratic society.

CONCLUSION

As visual representations of students' thought processes, graphic organizers have many applications related to instruction and assessment. In this chapter we have identified just a few of the many graphic organizers that may be used to instruct and assess different aspects of information literacy. In particular, we have described organizers that may be used to document achievement of the following goals related to information literacy:

- Explore different aspects of a topic
- Develop a global view of the topic
- Pose questions related to the topic
- Organize notes around research questions
- Compare and contrast topics and ideas
- Connect isolated pieces of information to create personal knowledge

In addition to these obvious benefits, we have found graphic organizers to be an effective way to differentiate learning for special needs children as well as those with language deficits. Graphic organizers allow these students to express ideas and make connections using signs, symbols, words, and phrases in place of rather sophisticated language constructions.

REFERENCES

Ausubel, David. 1967. *Learning Theory and Classroom Practice*. Ontario: The Ontario Institute for Studies in Education.

Bellanca, James. 1992. *The Cooperative Think Tank: Graphic Organizers to Teach Thinking in the Cooperative Classroom*. Palantine, Ill.: Skylight Publishing.

Callison, Daniel. 2003. *Key Words, Concepts and Methods for Information Age Instruction: A Guide to Teaching Information Inquiry*. Baltimore, Md.: LMS Associates.

Ekhaml, Leticia. 1998. "Graphic Organizers: Outlets for Your Thoughts," *School Library Media Activities Monthly* 14, no. 5 (January): 29–33.

Enchanted Learning Software. 2004. *Zoom Rainforests*. URL: http://www.enchantedlearning.com/subjects/rainforest (accessed February 27, 2004).

Inspiration Software, Inc. n.d. *Kidspiration*. URL: http://www.inspiration.com/vlearning/index.cfm?fusaction=concept_maps (accessed February 27, 2004).

Marzano, Robert J., Jane E. Pollock, and Debra J. Pickering. 2001. *Classroom Instruction That Works: Research-Based Strategies for Increasing Student Achievement*. Alexandria, Va.: Association for Supervision and Curriculum Development.

National Endowment for the Humanities. n.d. *Portrait of a Hero: EDSITEment Lesson Plan*. URL: http://edsitement.neh.gov/view_lesson_plan.asp?id=262 (accessed January 29, 2004).

North Central Regional Educational Laboratory. 1995. *K-W-L-H Technique*. Adapted from *Strategic Teaching and Reading Project Guidebook*. URL: http://www.ncrel.org/sdrs/areas/issues/students/learning/lr1wlh.htm (accessed January 28, 2004).

Novak, Joseph. n.d. *The Concept Mapping Homepage*. URL: http://users.edte.utwente.nl/lanzing/cm_home.htm (accessed January 25, 2004).

Ogle, Doris S. 1986. "K-W-L Group Instructional Strategy." In *Teaching Reading as Thinking*, ed. A1 S. Palinesar, Doris S. Ogle, Beau F. Jones, and E. G. Carr. Alexandria, Va.: Association for Supervision and Curriculum Development, pp. 11–17.

Pappas, Marjorie. 1997. "Organizing Research," *School Library Media Activities Monthly* 14, no. 4 (December): 30–32.

Vandergrift, Kay E. 1994. *Power Teaching: A Primary Role for the School Library Media Specialist*. Chicago, Ill.: American Library Association.

Willson, Kathleen. n.d. *Concept Mapping and Inspiration*. The Virtual Institute. URL: http://www.ettc.net/techfellow/inspir.htm (accessed February 11, 2005).

CHAPTER 6

Beginning with the End in Mind: Elementary Grade Example

This chapter:

- Reviews an outcome-based strategy to lesson planning
- Presents a sample project in an elementary school setting
- Describes outcome-based planning for sample library lessons related to the project

OUTCOME-BASED APPROACH

In Chapter 2 we briefly discussed the importance of planning units and lessons with the end target in mind. The essential question is, what are students expected to demonstrate as a result of the learning experience? Assessment must directly measure how well students accomplish the desired outcome. The lesson plan or instructional procedure should be

Figure 6.1
Conventional versus outcome-based planning

Conventional Planning	Outcome-Based Planning
Start with ideas for activities	Start with a standard and a related performance indicator
Select an activity for the lesson	Define the learning task based on a performance indicator
Develop the lesson procedure	Determine the criteria to assess student performance Design a tool or method to do the assessment
Determine the lesson objectives based on a lesson activity Decide on an assessment technique (often viewed as ancillary and optional)	Develop an instructional procedure that is directly connected to the learning task and assessment

based on the intended target. As mentioned earlier, Wiggins and McTighe (1998) refer to this as "backward planning" since it begins with the end in mind. This is counter to common practice where instructors begin by creating lesson procedures and then tacking on objectives. In this latter type of planning, assessment is frequently ignored. Figure 6.1 displays the differences between the two approaches.

In Chapters 6, 7, and 8, we focus on how lessons implemented in the library media center might demonstrate an outcome-based approach to student learning. In this chapter we share library lessons that might be part of a classroom project in an elementary school. In Chapters 7 and 8 we apply the same outcome-based approach to lessons in middle and high school settings. The organization of all three chapters is identical. First, the project itself is summarized. This is followed by two sample lessons, each organized under the following major headings:

Outcomes: What must students be able to demonstrate at the end?

Standards and performance indicators addressed

Learning tasks related to performance indicators

Assessment: How will student performance be measured?

Criteria for assessment

Tool or method for assessment

Instructional procedure: How will this lesson be delivered?

What will instructors do?

What will students do?

Our examples are based on the assumption that there is some degree of cooperation or collaboration between library media specialists and teachers. The outcome-focused approach to lesson planning is most effective when teaching in the library media center is directly aligned with the learning targets of the classroom.

SUMMARY OF PROJECT

A third-grade class is studying about the wetlands. Early on, students decide they want to produce their own books with the information gathered. Their essential question is project-focused: What is important to share about wetlands? Where might we find this information?

To stimulate their curiosity, instructors take students on virtual tours of the Everglades, the Okefenokee Swamp, and the Louisiana coastal marshes. The students deepen their knowledge by participating in a field trip to a nearby wetlands area where they photograph and take notes on what they see and hear. Back in school they comb through trade books, encyclopedias, and the Internet to find additional information about the plants and animals they encountered on their field experience. Students eventually share their completed works at an authors' showcase in the library media center where they celebrate their accomplishments with families and other third-grade classes.

SAMPLE LESSONS

How might the library media specialist contribute to this project? We suggest two possibilities in this chapter and invite readers to think of other lessons that might be integrated into this unit:

- Lesson 1: Finding information in a variety of sources
- Lesson 2: Developing criteria to assess student books

Lesson 1: Finding Information in a Variety of Sources

In the classroom children create webs and generate questions to guide the search for information. At this point, the library media specialist steps in to help students with the task of identifying potential information sources. The objective of this lesson is to locate a variety of print and electronic sources to use in the project.

Outcomes Desired

Standards and Performance Indicators Addressed

This information is presented in Figure 6.2.

Learning Task Related to Performance Indicator

Students will explore different information centers in the library media center using a matrix to evaluate potential sources. The matrix will indicate the title of the resource, the type of information provided, and something that was learned about the topic.

Assessment

Criteria for Assessment

The criteria outlined in Figure 6.3 are used to assess students' ability to locate and use a variety of resources.

Figure 6.2
Standards and performance indicators addressed in lesson 1

Content Areas	Standards	Performance Indicators
Information Literacy	The student who is information literate accesses information efficiently and effectively (AASL and AECT 1998)	Identifies a variety of potential sources of information (AASL and AECT 1998)
Language Arts	The student gathers and uses information for research purposes (Kendall and Marzano 2004, online)	Uses electronic media to gather information Uses keywords, guide words, alphabetical and numerical order, indexes, cross-references, and lettered volumes to find information for research topics (Kendall and Marzano 2004, online)
Science	Science as inquiry: The student develops: • Abilities necessary to do scientific inquiry • Understanding about scientific inquiry Life science: The student develops understanding of: • The characteristics of organisms • The life cycles of organisms • Organisms and environments (National Research Council, n.d., online)	Employs simple equipment and tools to gather data and extend the senses Develops skills in the use of computers and calculators for conducting investigations Demonstrates an understanding of the following principle: An organism's patterns of behavior are related to the nature of its environment, including: • The kinds and numbers of other organisms present • The availability of food and resources • The physical characteristics of the environment (National Research Council, n.d., online)

Figure 6.3
Criteria for locating and using a variety of sources

- Locate information in at least three different resources.

- Access information in both print and electronic formats.

- Explain the kind of information found in different resources.

- State at least one thing learned from each resource.

Figure 6.4
Matrix for identifying resources

RESOURCE MATRIX

Link to the standards: In this lesson I will show that I can find information about my topic in different kinds of print and electronic resources.

The topic of my book is _____.

My research questions are

_____
_____
_____

The keywords I will use to search are _____.

Source of Information (Title)	Type of Information (Format)	One important thing I learned from the source

This best source that I found was _____

The reason I think this is _____

Tool or Method for Assessment

Teachers provide technical assistance as third graders visit the different information centers (e.g., OPAC, magazine database, electronic encyclopedias, print reference shelf, and the Internet). Figure 6.4 illustrates the matrix used by students as they survey resources to identify those that will be most useful for their projects. Students also use their learning logs to reflect on the experience and identify the resources they will examine for additional information.

Instructional Procedure

This lesson familiarizes students with the various information centers that have been set up in the library for them to identify potential sources for their projects. Figure 6.5 outlines the steps taken by instructors and students as they pursue this goal.

Figure 6.6 provides a visual map of the tools and resources available at each information center.

Lesson 2: Developing Criteria to Assess Student Books

The library media specialist undertakes the development of assessment criteria with the students as part of a bookmaking workshop. While the classroom teacher focuses on the writing process and the artwork, the library media specialist helps students understand how books are put together.

Outcomes Desired

Standards and Performance Indicators Addressed

This information is presented in Figure 6.7.

Learning Task Related to Performance Indicator

Students will develop a list of criteria to guide and assess the bookmaking project. The criteria will define quality indicators for writing, artwork, and overall presentation.

Assessment

Criteria for Assessment

Students will assist in identifying the criteria to assess their books. Figure 6.8 is an example of what the criteria might look like.

Figure 6.5
Instructional procedure for identifying information sources

What Will Instructors Do?	What Will Students Do?
Suggest questions that could be used to focus the search for information on a wetlands animal. Examples: • What are the wetlands? • What plants and animals live in the wetlands? • Why are the wetlands a threatened habitat? • How can we help to save the wetlands? Ask students how we can find the answers to our questions? Where can we look?	Review the questions they have written for their books about the wetlands. Brainstorm a list of possible resources.
Use students' responses to create a map showing the information centers in the library and what can be found at each. (See Figure 6.6)	Participate in the discussion leading to the creation of a map of library resources. (Figure 6.6)
Explain the matrix.	Write topic on the matrix. Identify alternative search words.
Provide technical assistance as students access resources. Assist students who need help filling in the matrix.	Visit each of the information centers. Use search words to access potential sources. Fill in information required by the matrix.
Assessment: The completed matrices will be analyzed. In addition, students will respond to the following prompts in their learning logs: • What problems did you have filling out your resource matrix? • Which resources do you think will be most helpful for your project? Why?	Students will refer to the matrix as they reflect on the experience and write their thoughts in their learning logs.

Figure 6.6
Map of library resources

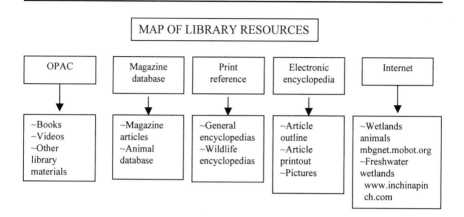

Figure 6.7
Standards and performance indicators addressed in lesson 2

Content Areas	Standards	Performance Indicators
Information Literacy	The student who is an independent learner is information literate and strives for excellence in information seeking and knowledge generation (AASL and AECT 1998)	Devises strategies for revising, improving, and updating self-generated knowledge (AASL and AECT 1998)
Language Arts	The student uses general skills and strategies of the writing process (Kendall and Marzano 2004, online)	Drafting and revising: Uses strategies to revise written work Editing and publishing: Uses strategies to publish written work Evaluates own and others' writing (Kendall and Marzano 2004, online)
Science	Life science: The student develops understanding of: • The life cycles of organisms • The characteristics of organisms • Organisms and environments (National Research Council n.d., online)	Demonstrates an understanding of the following principle: An organism's patterns of behavior are related to the nature of its environment, including: • The kinds and numbers of other organisms present • The availability of food and resources • The physical characteristics of the environment (National Research Council n.d., online)

Figure 6.8
Criteria for evaluating student books

Writing
- Content—It provides important information about the topic.
- Organization—There is a beginning, a middle, and an end.
- Voice—It is written in the author's own words.
- Sentence fluency—It is written in complete sentences that flow naturally.
- Word choice—Words are carefully chosen to represent the wetlands accurately.
- Conventions—There are no mistakes in spelling, grammar, or punctuation.

Artwork
- The pictures show the wetlands accurately.
- The pictures and the text go together.
- Color, design, and composition are used creatively.

Overall presentation
The book has the following parts:
- An attractive cover.
- A title page that has the title of the book, the author's name, the publisher's name, and the place of publication.
- At least four pages containing text and illustrations.
- A list of resources.
- Something about the author.

Tool or Method for Assessment

Instructors and students devise a checklist that reflects the criteria they have established (Figure 6.9). In addition, students write in their learning logs about what they think are the most important things to keep in mind as they create their books.

Instructional Procedure

This particular lesson focuses on helping students to identify criteria to assess their books. The library media specialist uses *A Wetland Walk*, by Sheri Amsel, to introduce this lesson. Figure 6.10 summarizes what instructors and students do to achieve the desired outcome.

CONCLUSION

The key to effective learning starts with students having a clear idea of what they must demonstrate. To measure how well students achieve the expected goal requires a careful delineation of criteria and the selection of an appropriate tool or strategy for the assessment. The instructional

Figure 6.9
Checklist for assessing Wetlands books

> <u>Link to the standards</u>: In this lesson I will learn how to improve my work by using a checklist to assess my writing, my artwork, and my book as a whole.

TITLE OF THE BOOK:_____

AUTHOR/ILLUSTRATOR: _____

Assessing Your Wetlands Book

Criteria—What's important?	Yes	No	Comments
WRITING			
Does it provide important information about the wetlands?			
Does it have a beginning, a middle, and an end?			
Is it written in the author's own words?			
Is it written in complete sentences that flow naturally?			
Are words carefully chosen to describe the sights and sounds of the wetlands?			
Are there any mistakes in spelling, grammar, or punctuation?			
ARTWORK			
Are the wetlands shown accurately in the pictures?			
Do the pictures and text go together?			
Are color, design, and composition used creatively?			
OVERALL PRESENTATION			
Do the words and pictures present the wetlands in an interesting way?			
Does the book have an attractive cover?			
Does the title page have the book's title, the names of the author and publisher, and the place of publication?			
Are there four or more pages with text and pictures about the wetlands?			
Is there a list of the resources used to find the information?			
Is there a part that tells something about the author?			

Figure 6.10
Instructional procedure for developing assessment criteria with students

What Will Instructors Do?	What Will Students Do?
Strategies for introducing the literature—Modeling and direct instruction Introduce *A Wetland Walk*. Call attention to: – The book cover – The title page – Pages with illustrated text – List of references – Information about the author Lead up to the questions: What do you think this book will be about? Will it be fiction or nonfiction? How do you know? Write responses on a chart.	Students draw upon their previous knowledge in responding to questions posed by instructor. Reading strategy—prediction Students make predictions about the contents of the book as well as the ideas that might be presented. Responses are recorded on a chart. Students' comments might include: – It's nonfiction because it gives information. – The pictures show what the wetlands are like. – It should tell about the things you see, hear, and feel in the wetlands. – It might explain why the wetlands are important.
Strategies for experiencing the literature—Shared reading, validation Guide the reading by referring to predictions: – What can you see, hear, feel, or touch as you listen? – What is the author's message? How does she get it across? – Does the book explain why the wetlands are important? Read aloud, stopping occasionally to check for understanding or to focus attention on a critical point.	Students demonstrate critical listening skills by responding to the reading and by participating in group discussion.

Figure 6.10 (*Continued*)

Strategies for responding to the literature—Small group interaction with feedback	

Summarize the discussion by asking students what *A Wetland Walk* has in common with other good books? Record responses on a chart under the headings: writing, artwork, and overall presentation:
 	
WHAT ARE THE QUALITIES OF A GOOD BOOK?
 	
Writing
 	
Artwork
 	
Overall presentation
	Students meet in small groups to discuss the qualities of a good book. They record their ideas on a handout modeled after the chart. Responses might include:
	
	Writing
	  – It sticks to the topic. Everything is about the wetlands.
	  – The words help you to see, hear, or feel what the wetlands are like.
	  – Everything on the page is about the same thing.
	  – There are no mistakes in spelling.
	
	Artwork
	  – The pictures and the words match.
	  – The pictures show plants and animals that belong in the wetlands.
	  – The pictures are well made.

The library media specialist uses student-generated criteria to create a checklist for assessing student-made books.	Overall presentation
	  – All the parts are there—title page, illustrations, list of sources, etc.
	  – The cover makes you want to read it.

Assessment: The handouts completed by each group will be examined to determine the overall success of the lesson. In addition, each student is asked to respond to the following learning log prompt: "As you work on your book about the wetlands, what do you think are the most important things to keep in mind?"	Students respond to the prompt in their learning logs. Their responses should include some reference to the quality of writing and art as well as the overall presentation.

Figure 6.11
Grade 3 project: Focus, outcome, task, and assessment tool

Lesson Focus	Desired Outcome	Learning Task	Assessment Tool
Lesson 1 Finding information in various sources	Be able to identify at least three different print and electronic sources	Explore various information sources and indicate titles, types of information found, and information learned about the topic	Matrix that requires documenting titles, types of information, and information learned about the topic
Lesson 2 Developing criteria to evaluate the final product	Be able to devise strategies for revising, improving, and updating self-generated knowledge	Develop a list of criteria to assess the student-made books on topics relating to the wetlands	Checklist for books that includes criteria for assessing the writing, artwork, and overall presentation

procedure is ultimately shaped by the targeted outcome. Figure 6.11 summarizes the key elements of the lessons in this chapter.

In the next chapter, we present a middle school example of how lessons taught in the library media center might reflect an outcome-based approach to instructional design.

REFERENCES

American Association of School Librarians, and Association for Educational Communications and Technology. 1998. *Information Power: Building Partnerships for Learning*. Chicago, Ill.: American Library Association.

Kendall, John S., and Robert J. Marzano. 2004. *Content Knowledge: A Compendium of Standards and Benchmarks for K-12 Education*. 4th edition. Aurora, Colo.: Mid-Continent Research for Education and Learning. URL: http://www.mcrel.org/compendium/skillsIntro.asp (accessed July 8, 2004).

National Research Council. n.d. *National Science Education Standards*. URL: http://www.nap.edu/readingroom/books/uses/html/ (accessed July 7, 2004).

Wiggins, Grant, and Jay McTighe. 1998. *Understanding by Design*. Alexandria, Va.: Association for Supervision and Curriculum Development.

CHAPTER 7

Beginning with the End in Mind: Middle School Example

This chapter:

- Reviews an outcome-based strategy to lesson planning
- Presents a sample project in a middle school setting
- Describes outcome-based planning for sample library lessons related to the project

In Chapter 6, we began with a description of outcome-based instruction and presented examples of lessons in an elementary grade project that were planned in that manner. We present more examples in this chapter, this time at the middle school level. We start with a summary of a classroom-library project and follow this with two related lessons that might be taught in the library media center. Each lesson is formatted as follows:

Outcomes: What must students be able to demonstrate at the end?

Standards and performance indicators addressed

Learning tasks related to performance indicators

Assessment: How will student performance be measured?

Criteria for assessment

Tool or method for assessment

Instructional procedure: How will this lesson be delivered?

What will instructors do?

What will students do?

SUMMARY OF PROJECT

When eighth graders read the stories of Anne Frank and other Holocaust victims, they react with dismay and disbelief. Their need to make sense of this tragic event leads to thoughtful questions that demand honest, if difficult, explanations. Recognizing the need for background information, English teachers solicit the help of the library media specialist who contributes to the project by suggesting additional pieces of literature and guiding students through the process of gathering information about this era in history. Two essential questions frame the study: "Why is it important to remember the Holocaust?" and "How can we apply the lessons of the Holocaust to our lives today?"

When the class suggests a Holocaust museum in the library media center to memorialize the victims of the tragedy, the instructors ask them to work in pairs to prepare their displays. The library media specialist helps the students in choosing a research focus, posing questions, identifying potential resources, and collecting information needed to prepare the exhibits.

SAMPLE LESSONS

We present two library-based lessons that are critical for this project:

- Lesson 1: Asking the right questions
- Lesson 2: Appreciating creative forms of expression

Lesson 1: Asking the Right Questions

Quality research begins with the right questions that serve as a guide for reading and note taking. They tell students what to look for as they survey resources. They help to define the topic by targeting the most important and relevant information in terms of both the topic and the product. Meaningful questions help students decide which resources to use, which notes to take, and how to organize the information for an effective presentation.

This library lesson seeks to determine: What is a good research question? How do we write one?

Outcomes Desired

Standards and Performance Indicators Addressed

This information is presented in Figure 7.1.

Learning Task Related to Performance Indicator

Students will write from three to five questions related to their research topics.

Assessment

Criteria for Assessment

As much as possible, criteria will be written in the words of the students. Accuracy, relevancy, and comprehensiveness must be reflected in the criteria. Figure 7.2 illustrates what student-generated criteria for questions might look like:

Figure 7.1
Standards and performance indicators addressed in lesson 1

Content Areas	Standards	Performance Indicators
Information Literacy	The student who is information literate accesses information efficiently and effectively (AASL and AECT 1998)	Formulates questions based on information needs (AASL and AECT 1998)
Language Arts	The student conducts research on issues and interests by generating ideas and questions and by posing problems (NCTE and IRA 1995, online)	Gathers data for research topics (e.g., asks relevant questions) (Kendall and Marzano 2004, online)
History	The student conducts historical research (National Center for History in the Schools 1996, online)	Formulates historical questions from encounters with historical documents, eyewitness accounts, letters, diaries, artifacts, photos, historical sites, art, architecture, and other records from the past (National Center for History in the Schools 1996, online)

Figure 7.2
Criteria for questions

Good research questions:

- Relate to the essential questions.

- Lead to important information about the topic.

- Ask "how" and "why" as well as "who," "what," "when," and "where."

- Encourage comparisons and connections.

- Target information needed to complete the project.

Tool or Method for Assessment

Instructors use the criteria to create a rubric that serves as a guide for self-assessment and provides a means to determine each student's level of proficiency in generating thoughtful questions. Before students embark upon the task of collecting information, they review their questions with an instructor using the rubric displayed in Figure 7.3. Questions are revised based upon this assessment.

Figure 7.3
Assessment rubric for generating questions

	Link to the standards: My goal for this lesson is to write questions that will focus the research on important information that will help with my project.

Exceeds standards	Research questions help answer the essential question. Questions target important facts and basic information about the topic. Some questions ask "how" and "why." All questions are clear and to the point. Questions call for comparisons or connections with other events in history. At least one question leads to visual information needed for the project.
Meets standards	The questions target important facts and basic information about the topic, but it is not clear how they answer the essential question. There is at least one question that asks "how" or "why." The questions are clear but may be too general. None of the questions call for comparisons or connections to be made. One question leads to visual information needed for the project.
Approaches standards	The questions ask "who," "what," "when," and "where." None of the questions ask "how" or "why." The point of some questions is not clear. The questions lead to a list of facts rather than a deeper understanding of the topic. None of the questions targets the need for visual information.

Instructional Procedure

The groundwork for this lesson was laid in the classroom where students have been reading fiction and nonfiction selections about the Holocaust including:

- Anne Frank's *The Diary of a Young Girl*—a memoir or personal narrative
- David Adler's *We Remember the Holocaust*—a history based on personal narratives
- Milton Meltzer's *Rescue: The Story of How Gentiles Saved Jews in the Holocaust*—historical accounts
- Ida Vos's *Hide and Seek*—a novel
- Hana Volavkova's *I Never Saw Another Butterfly: Children's Drawings and Poems*—a collection of artwork and poetry by children of the Holocaust

The library media specialist draws upon insights students have gained through the literature to provide a purpose and a focus for the research. Figure 7.4 outlines the instructional procedure used to help students develop their questions.

Figure 7.4
Instructional procedure for lesson on generating questions

What Will Instructors Do?	What Will Students Do?
Strategies for introducing the lesson—Tap prior knowledge by asking questions: • What do you know about the Holocaust? • What questions do you have? • Why is it important to learn about the Holocaust? • How do you think we can learn more about it?	Students meet in existing literature circles to work on the first column of a K-W-L chart. They brainstorm what they know about the Holocaust based upon the literature. The class compares K-W-L charts and discusses why it is important to learn more and where the information can be found.
Strategies for developing a research focus • Remind students that questions might be used to focus the research. • Ask students to share some of the questions they have about the Holocaust.	Students meet again in literature circles to work on column two of the K-W-L chart—What do we want to find out about the Holocaust? Questions might include: • Why do we remember the Holocaust? • Why didn't the Nazis like the Jews? • How is Hitler connected to the Holocaust? • What was life like for the Jewish people before the war? During the war? • What is anti-Semitism? How is it related to the Holocaust? • Who besides Jews were victims of the Holocaust? • What is meant by "the final solution"? • What happened in the death camps?
Explain how questions guide the search for information. Differentiate between: • Essential questions for the unit • A broad question that provides a research focus • More specific questions that guide the search for information	

(*Continued*)

Figure 7.4 (*Continued*)

Provide a model showing a hierarchy of questions:
 	
Essential questions for the unit:
   • Why is it important to remember the Holocaust?
   • How do the lessons of the Holocaust affect us today?
Focus question: What was the Holocaust?
Questions to guide the information search:
Where did it happen?
When did it happen?
Who was involved?
What happened to these people?
How was the world changed by this event?
Why is it important to remember the victims?
What other events in history can it be compared with?
	Using the questions modeled by the instructors and those on their K-W-L charts, students consider the criteria for good research questions. Each group selects five criteria to share with the class. After discussing all of the suggestions, the class comes to a consensus on the criteria for good research questions.
	
	Students use this list along with the questions they have generated to brainstorm the criteria for good research questions.

Instructors use the criteria to develop a rubric for research questions.	Students develop from three to five research questions.
Instructors confer with students individually using the rubric to review their questions.	Students use the rubric (see Figure 7.3) to revise their questions.

Lesson 2: Appreciating Creative Forms of Expression

Lesson two combines the teaching role of the library media specialist with that of the resource provider. In this dual capacity, he or she assists with resources for learning, presents them in a way that is attractive and meaningful, and helps students analyze and compare what they read, see, and hear.

Outcomes Desired

Standards and Performance Indicators Addressed

This information is presented in Figure 7.5.

Learning Task Related to Performance Indicator

From a list of Holocaust resources, students will select three titles to read or view independently. The three items they choose must represent

Figure 7.5
Standards and performance indicators addressed in lesson 2

Content Areas	Standards	Performance Indicators
Information Literacy	The student who is an independent learner is information literate and appreciates literature and other creative expressions of information (AASL and AECT 1998)	Derives meaning from information presented creatively in a variety of formats (AASL and AECT 1998)
Language Arts	The student reads a wide range of literature from many periods and in many genres to develop an understanding of the dimensions of human experience (NCTE/IRA 1995, online)	Uses reading skills and strategies to understand a variety of literary passages and texts Understands point-of-view in a literary text (Kendall and Marzano 2004, online)
History	The student conducts historical research (National Center for History in the Schools 1996, online)	Obtains historical data from a variety of sources, including: library and museum collections, historic sites, historical photos, journals, diaries, eyewitness accounts, newspapers, and the like; documentary films, oral testimony from living witnesses, censuses, tax records, city directories, statistical compilations, and economic indicators (National Center for History in the Schools 1996, online)

different genres and formats, e.g., a memoir, a play, and a video. Using a matrix, they will analyze each of these creative expressions on the basis of the point of view represented, the information provided, and the overall treatment of the topic.

Assessment

Criteria for Assessment

The purpose of the assignment is to provide guidelines for students to derive meaning from information presented in various formats. The criteria presented in Figure 7.6 will be used to measure achievement.

Figure 7.6
Criteria for deriving meaning from information presented in different formats

---

- Uses a variety of information sources to build an understanding of the topic.

- Identifies the point of view in the piece selected.

- Evaluates the strengths and weaknesses of a particular creative expression.

- Explains how a book, play, video, or poem has contributed to one's personal understanding of the event.

Tool or Method for Assessment

Students will use a response sheet (Figure 7.7) to analyze each of their selections. They complete separate response sheets for three selections. The final score represents an average of the three responses.

Instructional Procedure

This lesson begins in the classroom where the assignment is made to select and read at least three creative pieces that provide information about the Holocaust experience. Prior to meeting with the class, the library media specialist compiles a list of videos, dramatic scripts, poetry collections, historical works, biographies, and novels available in the media center. Figure 7.8 outlines the instructional procedure used in the library media center to support the learning.

CONCLUSION

In both Chapters 6 and 7 we have provided examples of lessons that might be integrated into existing classroom projects. In each case, library media specialists begin the lesson construction process with careful attention to what students need to demonstrate by the end of the learning experience. They clearly delineate criteria to assess the quality of student performance and the task that allows students to show how well they have learned the targeted concept or skill. The assessment tools are designed with the targets in mind. Figure 7.9 summarizes the key elements of the lessons in this chapter.

In the next chapter, we present a high school example of how lessons taught in the library media center might reflect an outcome-based approach to instructional design.

Figure 7.7
Tool for responding to literature in multiple formats and genres

Link to standards: I will gain a deeper understanding of the Holocaust by reading and responding to a variety of literary pieces presented in different formats.

AUTHOR OR PERSON RESPONSIBLE:
_____

TITLE: _____

FORMAT OR GENRE: _____

QUESTIONS	MY THOUGHTS	EVIDENCE FROM THE WORK
From whose point-of-view is the story told?		
How did the piece contribute to my understanding of the Holocaust?		
What did I like best about this piece?		
What did I like least about this piece?		
How does it compare to other things I have read or viewed about the Holocaust?		

Figure 7.8
Instructional procedure for responding to creative forms of expression

What Will Instructors Do?	What Will Students Do?
Introductory activity: Compare a segment from the DVD "Anne Frank Remembered" with book being read in class. • Refer to "Diary of a Young Girl." • Ask how the DVD might compare with the book. • Show a ten-minute segment.	Use a T-chart to jot down similarities and differences while viewing. Similarities Differences
Synthesize the discussion around points made by students. These may include: • The same situation is presented in both. • The author of the book tells the story in her own words. • The video gives an outsider's point-of-view. • The book tells the story with words. • The video uses pictures and sound to tell the story.	Form groups to discuss the DVD and compare charts. Summarize discussion for the class.
Read a poetry selection related to the Holocaust (e.g., "Daniel" by Laura Crist available at www.mtsu.edu/~baustin/daniel.html)	Discuss in groups the poem's treatment of the Holocaust experience. Does the poem contribute to our understanding? How?
Review the assignment: • Read at least three selections in different formats and genres. • Complete a response form for each selection. Provide students with a list of Holocaust resources available in the library media center. Briefly comment on each piece calling attention to the genre, the format, and other features that may affect selection.	Select three or more items from the list. Read or view each of the items.
Explain the response form.	Complete a response form for each item.
Use response forms to assess learning. Provide students with feedback.	Make adjustments based upon feedback.

Figure 7.9
Grade 8 unit: Focus, outcome, task, and assessment tool

Lesson Focus	Desired Outcome	Learning Task	Assessment Tool
Lesson 1 Generating questions	Be able to formulate questions based on information needs	Generate 3 to 5 questions related to students' research areas	Rubric that identifies the quality of questions based on requirements of accuracy, relevance, and scope
Lesson 2 Responding to literature	Be able to derive meaning from information presented in a range of formats	Read and respond to 3 different literary pieces presented in 3 different formats	Literary response sheet that requires analysis of points of view, information provided, and overall presentation

REFERENCES

American Association of School Librarians, and Association for Educational Communications and Technology. 1998. *Information Power: Building Partnerships for Learning*. Chicago, Ill.: American Library Association.

Kendall, John S., and Robert J. Marzano. 2004. *Content Knowledge: A Compendium of Standards and Benchmarks for K-12 Education*. 4th edition. Aurora, Colo.: Mid-Continent Research for Education and Learning. URL: http://www.mcrel.org/compendium/skillsIntro.asp (accessed July 8, 2004).

National Center for History in the Schools. 1996. *National Standards for History: Grades 5-12*. URL: http://www.sscnet.ucla.edu/nchs/standards/thinking 5-12-4.html (accessed July 7, 2004).

National Council of Teachers of English, and International Reading Association. 1995. *Standards for the English Language Arts*. URL: http://www.readwritethink. org/standards/(accessed July 6, 2004).

CHAPTER 8

Beginning with the End in Mind: High School Example

This chapter:

- Reviews an outcome-based strategy to lesson planning
- Presents a sample project in a high school setting
- Describes outcome-based planning for sample library lessons related to the project

In Chapters 6 and 7 we presented examples of lessons that library media specialists incorporated into elementary and middle school projects. In each instance, we demonstrated how effective lesson planning starts with the careful identification of information literacy standards and related performance indicators that target specific learning outcomes. With these outcomes as the focus, library media specialists then determined how to assess student performance and how to shape the learning experience to help students achieve the desired outcomes.

The sample lessons in this chapter are part of a high school Senior Project assignment. As we did in the earlier chapters we begin with a summary of the overall project and follow this with two related lessons that might be taught in the library media center. Each lesson is formatted as follows:

Outcomes: What must students be able to demonstrate at the end?

Standards and performance indicators addressed
Learning task related to performance indicator

Assessment: How will student performance be measured?

Criteria for assessment
Tool or method for assessment

Instructional procedure: How will this lesson be delivered?

What will instructors do?
What will students do?

SUMMARY OF PROJECT

The Senior Project is becoming as much a part of the high school land-scape as SATs, GPAs, and commencement exercises. Many schools have adopted it as a way for students to demonstrate their competencies through an in-depth study of a topic of their choice.

Proponents of the Senior Project describe it as a culminating activity that allows students to apply what they have learned to a project that is personally meaningful. By providing opportunities to develop and polish a range of skills and aptitudes, it prepares high school graduates for college and the workplace. Properly implemented, the Senior Project has the potential of "transforming the senior year into one of challenge, engagement, and high-quality learning" (Egelson 2002).

Senior Projects promote the goals of information literacy by engaging students in a process that involves producing, applying, and communicating knowledge. Typically, students are teamed with a mentor who helps them set goals, generate questions, locate sources, and design a method of investigation. They share their findings through research papers, science experiments, multimedia presentations, and a host of other products and performances. As they work on their projects, students are engaged in a continuous stream of reflection, revision, and self-discovery (O'Grady 1999).

Although districts have set different guidelines for fulfilling the Senior Project requirement, most schools see the project as a vehicle for students to demonstrate learning by (Egelson 2002, Martin 2001):

- Showing what they know and are able to do
- Engaging in a focused investigation related to an area of interest or a career choice
- Using an inquiry process to build knowledge and understanding
- Utilizing feedback to revise and improve their work
- Preparing and presenting findings to a panel of judges

SAMPLE LESSONS

At one high school, teachers begin the year with an informational meeting to explain the project and to address the questions and concerns of students and their parents. During the meeting three components of the project are identified and described. These include:

- a research paper on a student-selected topic
- a project that has a logical connection to the research
- a presentation before a panel of judges representing the faculty, the student body, and the larger community

Teachers, counselors, and volunteers from the community serve as mentors and seminar leaders helping students with specific tasks related to the project. The library media specialist participates by offering instruction on critical aspects of the research process. Two of the lessons that prove to be most successful are:

- Lesson 1: Evaluating web sites
- Lesson 2: Preparing an annotated bibliography

Lesson 1: Evaluating Web Sites

Teachers work with the library media specialist to develop guidelines for the research component of the project. Considerable emphasis is placed on the selection, evaluation, and use of both print and electronic resources. However, early in the process, it becomes evident that many students are relying on the Internet to the exclusion of other information sources. Teachers also observe that students are selecting sites indiscriminately without regard to issues of accuracy, reliability, or relevance. In response to these concerns the library media specialist designs a lesson focusing on web site evaluation.

Outcomes Desired

Standards and Performance Indicators Addressed

The information is presented in Figure 8.1.

Figure 8.1
Standards and performance indicators addressed in lesson 1

Content Areas	Standards	Performance Indicators
Information Literacy	The student who is information literate evaluates information critically and competently (AASL and AECT 1998)	Determines accuracy, relevance, and comprehensiveness Identifies inaccurate and misleading information Selects information appropriate to the problem or question at hand (AASL and AECT 1998)
Language Arts	The student conducts research on issues and interests by generating ideas and questions and by posing problems. The student gathers, evaluates, and synthesizes information from a variety of sources (NCTE and IRA 1995, online)	Uses a variety of criteria to evaluate the validity and reliability of primary and secondary sources (Kendall and Marzano 2004, online)
Additional Content Standards	Standards and performance indicators for other content areas should be included here depending on the focus of the student projects.	

Learning Task Related to Performance Indicator

Students will select three web sites as information sources for their projects. They will evaluate these sites using a tool developed for that purpose.

Assessment

Criteria for Assessment

Students participate in setting the criteria for evaluating web sites. They are written in the language of students and focus on content, authority, and presentation. Figure 8.2 lists examples of the criteria.

Tool or Method for Assessment

The library media specialist uses the criteria developed with students to design a rating scale for web site evaluation (Figure 8.3). Students use this tool to evaluate web sites dealing with their topics. In addition, they respond in their learning logs to the following prompts: Why is it important to evaluate web sites? What are some ways of finding out more about the author, the content, or the purpose of the web site? Responses to these questions are attached to the rating sheets and used as a basis for assessment and further instruction.

Figure 8.2
Criteria for evaluating web sites

Content
- Information is accurate and complete.
- Information is related to the topic and helps answer the research questions.
- Both sides of the issue are presented.
- The reading level is neither too hard, nor too easy.
- The information is current. Dates of publication and the last update are given.
- The information will be helpful for this project.

Authority/credibility
- The person or organization responsible for the information is stated.
- The URL indicates that the sponsor is a government agency, an academic institution, or an organization with a reputation in the field.
- There is no obvious bias for or against a particular point of view.
- The purpose of the page is to inform or explain—not to entertain, sell a product, or influence public opinion.

Presentation and ease of use
- The page loads easily.
- The links are easy to use.
- Topics, headings, and bullets are used to break up the text.
- Graphics, artwork, and other features enhance the presentation and contribute to understanding.
- There are no obvious errors in spelling, grammar, or other conventions.

Figure 8.3
Tool for assessing web sites

WEB SITE EVALUATION TOOL

Link to the standards: I will use criteria for accuracy, relevance, completeness, and ease of use to evaluate web sites to use in my project.

Name of Web Site: _____   URL: _____

	Lacking	Satisfactory	Excellent
Content			
Does the information appear to be accurate?			
Is the coverage of the topic comprehensive?			
Does the information relate to your topic and questions?			
Are different points of view represented?			
Is the reading level appropriate for you?			
Is the information current? (Check the last update usually found at the bottom of the page.)			
Will the information help with your project?			
Authority/credibility			
Is the name of the author or sponsoring organization stated?			
Is the author qualified to speak on the topic?			
Is the writing free of bias?			
Is the purpose to explain or provide information, rather than to sell or influence public opinion?			
Presentation and ease of use			
Does the page load easily?			
Are links provided to appropriate web sites? Are they active?			
Are topics, headings, and bullets used to break up the text?			
Do graphics, artwork, and other features enhance the presentation and contribute to understanding?			

Instructional Procedure

The purpose of the lesson is twofold: 1) to establish guidelines for evaluating web sites and 2) to have students use the rating scale to evaluate web sites. Figure 8.4 describes the procedure used to develop competency in web site evaluation.

Figure 8.4
Instructional procedure for evaluating web sites

What Will Instructors Do?	What Will Students Do?
Strategies for introducing the lesson: Tap prior knowledge Ask: What makes a web site useful for research? How do you choose one site over another on the same topic?	Students offer their ideas about what makes a good web site. Responses might include: • It's easy to use. • It has good information. • It answers your questions. • It includes pictures and graphics.
Strategies for building knowledge: Modeling, group interaction Use a scenario like the following one: Students are asked to write in their journals about their areas of interest, their hobbies and career goals. One student writes that he has two compelling interests—baseball and architecture. He thinks he might focus his research on baseball stadiums. For his project he wants to create a photo gallery with pictures, maps, architectural drawings, and other interesting information about historic ballparks. He begins his search for information by doing an Internet search using the keywords "baseball stadiums."	
The librarian presents a list of web sites along with brief descriptions of items retrieved for "baseball stadiums." She asks: Which of these sites are likely to answer the student's essential question: "What do historic stadiums say about the history of baseball?"	Students meet in small groups to examine the list and predict what the theme and scope of each will be. They predict the sites most likely to help with the essential question and report their findings to the class.
Follow-up question: How can you tell if the information is accurate when just about anyone can put up a web site?	Students offer ideas on how accuracy can be determined. Suggestions might include: • Check it out in a print source or

(*Continued*)

Figure 8.4 (*Continued*)

	another Internet site. • See if the author is an expert. • Look at the domain name to see what kind of site it is.
Call attention to URLs and domain names. Ask: What do these indicators mean? How might the domain name help you predict the usefulness of the page? Synthesize discussion by sharing examples of web sites with different domain indicators.	Students identify the following domain indicators: com, edu, gov, and org. They discuss the connection between the domain name and the purpose and content of the site.
Strategies for involving students in development of criteria: Direct instruction, group interaction with feedback Provide each group with printouts downloaded from web sites retrieved through a search for "baseball stadiums." Include one printout for each student. Printouts may be from sites like the following: • Baseball Hall of Fame http://www.baseballhalloffame.org • The Atlanta Photojournalism Seminar: Major League Baseball Stadiums http://www.photojournalism.org/baseball.html • Fairness of Major League Baseball Stadiums http://students.imsa.edu/ • Major League Baseball Stadium and Ballpark Photo Gallery http://www.digitballparks.com Provide directions for group activity. Synthesize discussion by asking: • Which sites give information about the history of the stadiums? • Which are most useful for the project? Why? • Which site deals with controversy about baseball stadiums? • Which sites do the best job of comparing the stadiums?	Group Activity • Distribute articles—one per student. • Identify URL and the domain indicator. • Predict the purpose and content of the page. • Read for information.

Figure 8.4 (*Continued*)

• How can we use domain names to determine the potential for a site? • What other factors should we consider in evaluating web sites?	• Discuss clues about purpose and content provided by URLs. • Suggest other factors to consider in selecting a web site for research.
Ask students to generate a list of questions to help with web site evaluation. Suggest that questions be organized around the categories of content, authority/credibility, and presentation/technical quality. Use questions to create a tool for evaluating web sites.	Group work: Students brainstorm a list of questions to use in evaluating web sites. Questions might include: • Who created the page? • What does the domain indicator tell us? • What is the purpose? • Does it address all sides of the issue? • When was it published? When was it last updated? • Is it easy to load? • Are there links to other pages? Do they work? • Is it easy to read and understand? • How does it compare with other sites on this topic?
Provide instructions for independent practice: • Locate three web pages for your research topic. • Rate each site using the assessment tool.	Independent practice: Students will • Search the web for information on their topics. • Select and print out three pages they think will help with their projects. • Use the rating scale to evaluate each web site.
Explain the learning log and its purpose.	Students write a response to the following prompt: Why is it important to evaluate web sites? What are some ways of finding out more about the author, the content, or the purpose of the site?
Use rating scales and responses to the prompt to determine how well the lesson meets its goal of setting criteria for website evaluation.	Use assessment feedback to become more efficient users of the Web.

Lesson 2: Preparing an Annotated Bibliography

An important requirement for the Senior Project is an annotated bibliography. This allows the library media specialist to assess several aspects of information literacy including the ability to locate, evaluate, and use information for a specific purpose. Although students have previous experience preparing bibliographies for their research papers, the library media specialist sees the Senior Project as an opportunity to assess aspects of information literacy related to the appropriate and ethical use of sources.

Outcomes Desired

Standards and Performance Indicators Addressed

The information is presented in Figure 8.5.

Learning Task Related to Performance Indicator

Students will write citations and annotations for at least three information sources representing different formats.

Assessment

Criteria for Assessment

Students brainstorm possible criteria to use with their bibliographies (Figure 8.6).

Figure 8.5
Standards and performance indicators addressed in lesson 2

Content Areas	Standards	Performance Indicators
Information Literacy	The student who contributes positively to the learning community and to society is information literate and practices ethical behavior in regard to information and information technology (AASL and AECT 1998)	Respects intellectual property rights (AASL and AECT 1998)
Language Arts	Students use a variety of technologies and information resources to gather and synthesize information and communicate knowledge (NCTE and IRA 1995, online)	Uses standard format and methodology for documenting reference sources (Kendall and Marzano 2004, online)

Figure 8.6
Criteria for assessing annotated bibliographies

- Includes citations for print, electronic, and personal resources.

- Uses a consistent style to properly cite each source.

- Follows conventions outlined in the style sheet provided.

- Makes evaluative statements that address relevance, authority, accuracy, and

 usefulness for the project in question.

Tool or Method for Assessment

The library media specialist uses the criteria that the students have contributed to develop a rubric for assessing annotated bibliographies (Figure 8.7).

Instructional Procedure

As students work on the research phase of their projects, they keep bibliographic records of the sources they use. This information provides a starting point for the lesson on annotated bibliographies. The lesson has two desired outcomes: students

- Follow conventions and use a consistent style to cite information sources
- Write an annotation for one of the sources

Figure 8.8 describes the instructional procedure used in the library media center to assist students with their bibliographic work.

CONCLUSION

Outcome-based learning and teaching challenges all instructors to consider dramatic shifts in both pedagogy and curriculum development practices (Luongo-Orlando 2003, Wiggins and McTighe 1998). It begins with establishing learning that focuses on standards, i.e., targeting goals, designing assessment tools, and selecting performance tasks based on the standards. Figure 8.9 summarizes the key elements of the lessons in this chapter.

Student engagement in self-assessment and reflection are essential in the learning process. In all the lessons presented, students question, contemplate, and determine the quality of their own work. By being partners

Figure 8.7
Rubric for assessing annotated bibliographies

Link to the standards: I will demonstrate respect for intellectual property rights by properly citing all of my information sources and by providing an annotation that shows how each source contributes to the project.

Criteria	Exceeds Standards	Meets Standards	Approaches Standards
Comprehensiveness	Cites more than three different kinds of sources.	Cites at least three different kinds of sources.	Cites fewer than three sources.
Citation style	All citations are complete. Observes conventions and uses a consistent style for citations.	Almost all citations are complete. Observes conventions. Style is not always consistent.	Almost all citations are incomplete. Does not follow a consistent style.
Summary of contents	Briefly describes the scope or the central theme of the source.	Gives specific information from the source rather than a summary of main ideas.	Lists some information found but does not attempt to summarize ideas.
Evaluation of source	Considers authority and expertise of the author(s). Points out strengths and weaknesses of source. Explains how the source helped with the project. Compares the item with other sources. Gives reasons for opinion.	Does not explain why the author is credible. Points out some strengths and weaknesses. Explains how the source helped with the project. Makes some statements comparing sources.	Does not consider expertise of author. Makes no attempt to point out strengths and weaknesses. Attempts to explain how a source helped with the project. Makes simple comparisons (e.g., good, better, best) without providing details.

in assessment, they critically examine the process and products of their efforts. They become more aware of the strengths and needed improvements in their work and determine the quality of their performances. Assessment in this context is not "assessing learning" but it truly becomes "assessing *for* learning."

Figure 8.8
Instructional procedure for developing bibliographies

What Will Instructors Do?	What Will Students Do?
Strategies used to introduce lesson: Tap prior knowledge through focused discussion. Ask: Why is a bibliography required for the project? Synthesize the discussion by making the following points about the reasons for a bibliography: • To demonstrate respect for intellectual property rights by crediting those responsible for the information • To validate the information presented	Group discussion Students offer their ideas on the need for a bibliography. Ideas might include statements like the following: • To show where you got the information • To give credit to the author • To prove that you didn't make it up • To back up your arguments • To show that you did your research
Pass out an example of a bibliography for students to compare with their list of resources. Ask: What is the difference between a list of resources and a bibliography?	Students work in groups to discuss the differences between a resource list and a bibliography. A T-chart is used to record responses. Resource List Bibliography
Provide copies of a style sheet to be used for Senior Projects. Explain the organization of the style sheet and how to use it to write citations. Provide guidance and feedback as students work on their citations.	Independent practice Students write citations for four sources: an article, a book, a personal interview, and an Internet web site.
Provide examples of annotated bibliographies. Ask: What is the purpose of the annotation in relation to the Senior Project? (An Internet search calls up several sites useful for teaching students about annotated bibliographies. We used the	Students offer their ideas on the purpose of the annotation. Comments might include: • It gives a general idea of what the item is about. • It tells why you picked this source. • It explains how the resource helped with your project.

(Continued)

Figure 8.8 (*Continued*)

University of Wisconsin's Writing Center available at http://www.wisc.edu/writing/Handbook/AnnotatedBibliography.html	• It compares the item with other sources you used or chose not to use.
Use students' comments to point out that the purpose of the annotation is to briefly summarize and evaluate the source.	Independent practice

Model the process:
Step one: Cite the item using the appropriate style.
Step two: Write one or two sentences to summarize the scope or theme of the item.
Step three: Write two or three evaluative sentences. These might:
  • Address the authority or credibility of the author(s)
  • Point out the strengths and weaknesses of the item
  • Explain how the source helped with the project
  • Compare the source with other items on the same topic
	Students use the process modeled by the library media specialist to write an annotation for one bibliographic item.

Use the rubric for assessing annotative bibliographies to provide feedback.	Use assessment feedback to create an annotated bibliography for their projects.

Figure 8.9
Senior project: Focus, outcome, task, and assessment tool

Lesson Focus	Desired Outcome	Learning Task	Assessment Tool
Lesson 1 Evaluating web sites	Be able to evaluate information critically and competently	Evaluate three web sites as appropriate information sources for their projects	Rating scale that includes analysis of the accuracy, relevance, and comprehensiveness of a web source
Lesson 2 Preparing annotated bibliographies	Be able to practice ethical behavior in regard to information use	Create citations and annotations for at least three information sources in different formats	Rubric that covers consistency and completeness in citations and evaluative annotations that reflect relevance, authority, and accuracy

REFERENCES

American Association of School Librarians, and Association for Educational Communications and Technology. 1998. *Information Power: Building Partnerships for Learning*. Chicago, Ill.: American Library Association.

Egelson, Paula. 2002. *Senior Project at SERVE*. URL: http://www.serve.org/senior project (accessed June 15, 2004).

Kendall, John S., and Robert J. Marzano. 2004. *Content Knowledge: A Compendium of Standards and Benchmarks for K-12 Education*. 4th edition. Aurora, Colo.: Mid-Continent Research for Education and Learning. URL: http://www. mcrel.org/compendium/skillsIntro.asp (accessed July 8, 2004).

Luongo-Orlando, Katherine. 2003. *Authentic Assessment: Designing Performance-Based Tasks*. Ontario, Canada: Pembroke Publishers Limited.

Martin, Patty. 2001. *Senior Project Institute: Institute Briefing Papers*. URL: http://www.sbe.wa.gov/reports/seniorproject.htm (accessed June 15, 2004).

National Council of Teachers of English, and International Reading Association. 1995. *Standards for the English Language Arts*. URL: http://www.readwrite think.org/standards/ (accessed July 6, 2004).

O'Grady, Alice. 1999. "Information Literacy Skills and the Senior Project," *Educational Leadership* 57, no. 2 (October): 61–62.

Wiggins, Grant, and Jay McTighe. 1998. *Understanding by Design*. Alexandria, Va.: Association for Supervision and Curriculum Development.

CHAPTER 9

Student Portfolios

This chapter addresses the following questions:

- What is a portfolio?
- What is an electronic portfolio?
- How do portfolios differ from other assessment tools?
- Why use portfolios?
- Who are the audiences for portfolios?
- How might the library media specialist use portfolios?
- What might a process folio look like?

WHAT IS A PORTFOLIO?

A portfolio is a collection of selected work samples that shows a picture of achievement over time. The components of the portfolio are carefully chosen to provide evidence of growth toward identified goals. The typical portfolio includes the following:

- Examples of student work
- Tools used to assess performance
- Evidence of reflection and self-examination

Taken together, these documents become the basis for meaningful communication involving students, parents, teachers, library media specialists, and other members of the instructional team.

Librarian involvement in portfolio systems is admittedly on the cutting edge. It is the next step to consider if library media specialists are already integrating information literacy skills with classroom assignments. To engage in this activity, they must be doing a fair amount of collaborative planning and teaching. The teachers must also be working on classroom student portfolios.

WHAT IS AN ELECTRONIC PORTFOLIO?

Electronic or e-portfolios allow students to digitize and store artifacts that use a range of technologies and multimedia elements. These might include images that have been scanned or produced with a digital camera, allowing for a mix of sound and video, as well as multimedia products using various authoring programs (e.g., HyperStudio, KidPix, Dreamweaver).

According to Tuttle (1997), the advantages of electronic over print portfolios include the following:

- Students can demonstrate more creative dimensions of learning, such as digitizing a speech or showing a movie or producing a web page on a project.
- Students can connect various portions of their portfolios through hyperlinks.
- New work can replace older work with minimal effort.
- There is no need to wade through a voluminous folder or a box of documents.
- E-portfolios definitely save space.

In addition, students might easily take their portfolios to another school or send them on to college or workplaces as part of their applications.

Before deciding whether to develop hard copy or electronic portfolios, however, Barrett (1997) cautions that schools consider the following factors:

- Computer skills of the teachers
- Computer skills of the students
- Access to computers by students and teachers
- Networking capacity in the school building and classrooms
- Budget for additional hardware and software
- Budget for staff development
- Resources for technical support
- Security and confidentiality of information stored in electronic form

It is not our intent to provide a detailed discussion of software and hardware that are needed to develop an e-portfolio system. For those schools interested in delving more deeply into the issues and requirements, we have appended a list of suggested readings at the end of this chapter.

HOW DO PORTFOLIOS DIFFER
FROM OTHER ASSESSMENT TOOLS?

Stiggins (1997) draws a clear distinction between portfolios and other assessment methods. He says that portfolios are collections of work that tell the whole story of student achievement. The purpose is to communicate

Figure 9.1
Portfolios versus other assessment measures

Characteristic	Portfolios	Other Assessments
Purpose	Show evolution of skills and knowledge	Assess specific targets in a specific time frame
Use	Communicate a range of achievement	Inform teaching and learning
Format	Include work samples, assessment tools, and reflections	Focus on specific assessment tools, including checklists, rubrics, rating scales, graphic organizers
Responsibility	Involve students, teachers, parents	Involve primarily teachers with students participating

"about student effort, growth, or achievement at any point in time" (Stiggins 1997, 79). Most assessment methods define the criteria for a successful performance in relation to specific learning targets. By contrast, the portfolio shows how learning grows and evolves across multiple projects and disciplines. The collection of work samples and assessment tools included in the portfolio provides a picture of learning that is authentic, integrated, and meaningful. Figure 9.1 highlights how portfolios differ from other forms of assessment.

WHY USE PORTFOLIOS?

Standards-based instructional programs require a more rigorous assessment of student performance. According to Mundell and DeLario (1994), portfolios provide a way to systematically assess the complex performances mandated by the standards. The outcome-based approach requires students to demonstrate what they know by working on tasks that involve decision-making, problem solving, and a range of skills and aptitudes. Portfolios are seen as an approach to assessment that is more in line with the emerging emphasis on process and authenticity in learning.

Many educators see portfolios as a way to complement the data provided by standardized tests. Combined with testing data, a carefully designed portfolio system provides a rich picture of student achievement that includes both qualitative and quantitative measures of learning.

When portfolios are designed to document the achievement of standards, they become an effective way of showing growth over time. Schools that use a process approach to instruction have found in portfolios a valuable tool for communication as well as assessment. Ideally, teachers, parents, and students use portfolios to engage in conversations about the *how* as well as the *what* of learning. In some schools students are trained to lead conferences with their parents and teachers by displaying their work samples, along with the tools used to assess them, and explaining the significance of each piece of evidence. The portfolio becomes the student's own story about learning.

WHO ARE THE AUDIENCES FOR PORTFOLIOS?

Different audiences review portfolios for different purposes. Figure 9.2 identifies how various members of the school community might use the information provided by portfolios.

Figure 9.2
Use of portfolios by different audiences

Audience	How Portfolio Is Used
Students	To self-examine growth as learners To communicate with others by displaying evidence of learning To value themselves as learners To provide a mechanism for sharing their products and experiences
Instructors	To monitor progress toward standards To plan interventions To modify teaching and learning
Parents	To monitor achievement To assess child's strengths and areas needing improvement To support the school's instructional program
Policy makers and other stakeholders	To supplement test data with qualitative measures of achievement To provide information needed to evaluate programs To make budgetary decisions To set policies and make decisions based on student achievement

HOW MIGHT THE LIBRARY MEDIA SPECIALIST USE PORTFOLIOS?

A form of the portfolio that is particularly useful for the library media specialist is the *process folio*. The process folio is a collection of student work that documents each phase of the learning process. Typically, it includes all the notes and drafts leading up to a final product or performance along with the tools used to assess the learning. Importantly, process folios also include reflections by the student on how he is learning, problems he is having, connections he is making, and how he feels about the entire process.

Because process folios focus on the process as well as the content of learning, they are an effective way of documenting complex tasks that involve a range of skills and aptitudes. By addressing all phases of the information search (Kuhlthau 1993), the process folio provides an excellent way to assess students' ability to access, manage, and use information. The following steps are crucial in developing a process folio:

1. Determine which standards will be the focus for instruction and assessment.
2. Develop tools and strategies to assess achievement of each standard.
3. Devise a consistent rating system for the assessment tools and strategies used.
4. Identify samples of student work to include for each standard.
5. Include selected samples of student reflections.
6. Prepare a summary sheet for the process folio.

WHAT MIGHT A PROCESS FOLIO INCLUDE?

On the following pages we describe how a student's process folio might be created for the Wetlands unit that we introduced in Chapter 6. As you recall, third graders investigated the topic through field trips as well as print and electronic resources. They ultimately authored books on their findings. In this third-grade project, the teacher used the process folio to collect achievement data for language arts and science while the library media specialist focused on the information search process.

The classroom teacher maintained the process folios for the duration of the third-grade year. When students worked in the library setting, they brought their process folios with them so that work samples, assessments, and reflections were properly filed and available to both the teacher and the library media specialist. Importantly, responsibility for maintaining the portfolios was shared by the instructors and the students.

Even students as young as third grade can be expected to help manage their process folios. With guidance from their instructors, these third graders were able to:

- Participate in setting criteria for quality work
- Assess their own learning
- Reflect upon what they were learning, how they were learning, and their reasons for selecting an item to put in their portfolios

The teacher was responsible for:

- Setting up and maintaining the process folios
- Monitoring the selection of items to be included
- Developing strategies and tools for assessing work samples
- Providing time for reflection and self-assessment
- Using the portfolio to communicate with parents

The library media specialist shared responsibility with the teacher for deciding what items to include in the process folio and developing tools and strategies for assessment. In undertaking this task, they followed the steps described below.

Step 1: Determine Standards That Are the Focus for Instruction and Assessment

In the Wetlands unit, the library media specialist decided to focus on the following two information literacy standards and their related performance indicators (AASL and AECT 1998):

- Standard 1: The student accesses information efficiently and effectively.

  Performance indicator 1: Formulates questions based on information needs.

  Performance indicator 2: Identifies a variety of information sources.

  Performance indicator 3: Uses successful strategies for accessing information.

- Standard 2: The student strives for excellence in information seeking and knowledge generation.

  Performance indicator 1: Assesses quality of process and products

  Performance indicator 2: Devises strategies for revising, improving, and updating self-generated knowledge.

A word of advice: While the instructor may be touching upon a number of standards in a particular unit, *it is wise to select a few standards (and performance indicators) that will be emphasized in direct instruction.* In other words, select only those standards that will actually be assessed. By establishing clear targets, the instructor also helps students stay on track.

Figure 9.3
Standards and assessment measures for Wetlands unit

Standard/Performance Indicators	Assessment Measure
Standard 1: The student accesses information efficiently and effectively.	
Performance indicator 1: Formulates questions based on information needs	Student-generated criteria for good questions Reflection log: What do I want to find out?
Performance indicator 2: Identifies a variety of information sources	Student-completed matrix for identifying resources
Performance indicator 3: Uses successful strategies for accessing information	Reflection log: How did I find information related to my questions?
Standard 2: The student strives for excellence in information seeking and knowledge generation.	
Performance indicator 1: Assesses quality of process and products	Student-completed checklist for bookmaking
Performance indicator 2: Devises strategies for revising, improving, and updating self-generated knowledge	Reflection log: What did I do to improve my book?

Step 2: Develop Tools and Strategies to Assess Achievement of Each Standard

For the Wetlands unit, the library media specialist created the following tools and strategies to assess student learning in relation to the two standards (Figure 9.3).

Step 3: Devise a Consistent Rating System for Assessment Tools Used

As shown in Figure 9.3, the library media specialist used several tools to assess student learning in this unit. To organize and make sense of the assessment data collected, it was important for her to devise a rating system that could be applied to assessment tools, such as matrices and checklists.

For the Wetlands unit, the library media specialist devised a four-level rating system (i.e., "exceeds," "meets," "approaches," and "does not meet" standards) that she used for the following assessment tools: (1) the matrix for identifying resources and (2) the checklist for bookmaking.

Figure 9.4
Matrix for identifying resources

Link to the standards: In this lesson I will show that I can find information about my topic in different kinds of print and electronic resources.

RESOURCE MATRIX

The topic of my book is _____.

My research questions are

_____

_____
_____

The keywords I will use to search are _____.

Source of Information (Title)	Type of Information (Format)	One important thing I learned from the source

The best source that I found was _____

The reason I think this is _____

Example A: Matrix for Identifying Resources

Figure 9.4 displays the matrix and Figure 9.5 shows the rating system as applied to the matrix.

Because significant value was placed on student involvement in the assessment process, the rating system was written from a student's perspective. Students used the rating system to assess their own resource matrices. Instructors reviewed each student's self-assessment and added their own comments. If there was a discrepancy between the student's evaluation and that of the teacher or library media specialist, a brief conference usually resulted in an agreement.

Figure 9.5
Rating system for matrix

Number of resources used	
Not met	I found only one resource for my topic.
Approaches	I found two resources for my topic.
Meets	I found three resources for my topic.
Exceeds	I found at least four resources for my topic.
Range of resources used	
Not met	I found only a print or an electronic resource.
Approaches	I found one print and one electronic resource.
Meets	I found more than one print and electronic resource.
Exceeds	I found print, electronic, and people resources.
Information found	
Not met	I didn't find anything to report.
Approaches	I reported something I learned from at least one resource.
Meets	I reported something I learned from each resource.
Exceeds	I reported something I learned from each resource. I also selected the best resource and told why I chose it.

Example B: Checklist for Bookmaking

Figure 9.6 displays the checklist and Figure 9.7 shows how the rating system was applied to this assessment tool.

Step 4: Identify Samples of Student Work to Include for Each Standard

For the Wetlands unit, the students included samples of their completed matrices and checklists.

Sample Work A: Completed Matrix

Figure 9.8 is an example of a student's matrix for identifying resources.

After completing her matrix, the student used the rating guide to assess her work. Instructors reviewed her self-assessment and added their own comments. In this particular case, the student decided that her resource matrix exceeded the standards and her instructors concurred with the student's assessment.

Sample Work B: Completed Checklist

This particular checklist was a handy tool for ongoing assessment of students' bookmaking skills. By using the checklist at critical intervals in the authoring process, the instructors were able to help students revise

Figure 9.6
Checklist for assessing Wetlands books

Link to the standards: In this lesson I will learn how to improve my work by using a checklist to assess my writing, my artwork, and my book as a whole._

TITLE OF THE BOOK:_____

AUTHOR/ILLUSTRATOR: _____

Assessing Your Wetlands Book

Criteria—What's important?	Yes	No	Comments
WRITING			
Does it provide important information about the wetlands?			
Does it have a beginning, a middle, and an end?			
Is it written in the author's own words?			
Is it written in complete sentences that flow naturally?			
Are words carefully chosen to describe the sights and sounds of the wetlands?			
Are there any mistakes in spelling, grammar, or punctuation?			
ARTWORK			
Are the wetlands shown accurately in the pictures?			
Do the pictures and text go together?			
Are color, design, and composition used creatively?			
OVERALL PRESENTATION			
Do the words and pictures present the wetlands in an interesting way?			
Does the book have an attractive cover?			
Does the title page have the book's title, the names of the author and publisher, and the place of publication?			
Are there four or more pages with text and pictures about the wetlands?			
Is there a list of the resources used to find the information?			
Is there a part that tells something about the author?			

Figure 9.7
Rating system for checklist

Writing	
Not met	My writing meets fewer than 2 of the criteria.
Approaches	My writing meets 2 or 3 criteria.
Meets	My writing meets 4 or 5 criteria.
Exceeds	My writing meets all 6 criteria.

Artwork	
Not met	My artwork does not meet any of the criteria.
Approaches	My artwork meets 1 of the criteria.
Meets	My artwork meets 2 of the criteria.
Exceeds	My artwork meets all 3 criteria.

Overall Presentation	
Not met	My overall presentation meets only 1 of the criteria.
Approaches	My overall presentation meets 2 or 3 criteria.
Meets	My overall presentation meets 4 or 5 criteria.
Exceeds	My overall presentation meets all 6 criteria.

and improve their work. Periodically, completed copies of the checklist were attached to drafts and submitted for review and feedback, thus providing a system for monitoring individual progress and planning meaningful instruction.

Figure 9.9 is an example of one student's final checklist for his book. The "X" indicated the student's self-assessment. After reviewing the student's rating and comments (S), the teacher (T) and library media specialist (L) added their own comments.

Looking over his final checklist, the student used the rating guide and indicated that he had met the standards for writing and artwork and that he exceeded the standard for the overall presentation. When asked how the checklist helped him to improve his work, the student responded:

This is the third time I filled in the checklist. I got better in everything except writing good sentences and my artwork. Even that is a little better, but I still don't understand composition. The checklist helped by telling me what was important, and the teachers' comments told me what I needed to do to get better. I'm glad I wasn't graded on my first try.

Step 5: Include Samples of Student Reflections

While a consistent rating system might be applied to a range of rubrics, checklists, matrices, and other graphic organizers, such a system would not be useful for examining reflection logs. Yet such logs contribute a

Figure 9.8
Example of student-completed matrix for identifying resources

Link to the standards: In this lesson I will show that I can find information about my topic in different kinds of print and electronic resources.

RESOURCE MATRIX

The topic of my book is _Dragonflies in the Wetlands._

My research questions are:
What do dragonflies look like?
What is their life cycle?
How have they adapted to life in the wetlands?

The keywords I will use to search are: dragonflies, insects, wetlands, ponds, and lakes

Source of Information (Title)	Type of Information (Format)	One important thing I learned from the source
Dragonflies (Wild Guide) by Cynthia Berger	_Book_	_I learned that dragonflies are "aerial hunters." (I wonder what that means.)_
Geokids—Tadpoles, Dragonflies, and Caterpillars	_Video_	_I learned that baby tadpoles, dragonflies, and caterpillars don't look like their parents._
Saving the Wetlands	_A web page_	_I learned that dragonflies are related to damselflies, stick bugs, water striders, and lots of other insects._
Dragonflies of the World by Jill Silsby	_Book_	_I learned that dragonflies are one of the oldest creatures on earth._

The best source that I found was _Dragonflies (Wild Guide)_

My reason for selecting this is: _It tells what dragonflies look like, how they hunt their food, and what their life cycle is like. It answers most of my questions and it has lots of pictures._

Figure 9.9
Example of student-completed checklist for assessing Wetlands books

Link to the standards: In this lesson I will learn how to improve my work by using a checklist to assess my writing, my artwork, and my book as a whole.

TITLE OF THE BOOK: *Call of the Canada Goose*
AUTHOR/ILLUSTRATOR: Sean

Assessing Your Wetlands Book

Criteria—What's important?	Yes	No	Comments
WRITING			
Does it provide important information about the wetlands?	X		*S: I included lots of important details about description, life cycle, and adaptation.* L: You answered all your questions.
Does it have a beginning, a middle, and an end?	X		T: Your introduction grabs attention and hints at what's to come.
Is it written in the author's own words?	X		*S: I used keywords and didn't copy.*
Is it written in complete sentences that flow naturally?		X	T: Much better, but we still need to work on this.
Are words carefully chosen to describe the sights and sounds of the wetlands?	X		L: I like phrases like "a round ball of down" and "hang out in meadowy places."
Are there any mistakes in spelling, grammar, or punctuation?		X	*S: I used the dictionary and asked my partner to double check.* T: Good strategy!
ARTWORK			
Are the wetlands shown accurately in the pictures?	X		L: The plants, animals, and landforms look like they belong in the wetlands.

Figure 9.9 (*Continued*)

Do the pictures and text go together?	X		*S: I read the text and then drew the pictures.*
Are color, design, and composition used creatively?		X	S:*I don't know how to do this.* T: We need more work on composition.
OVERALL PRESENTATION			
Do the words and pictures present the wetlands in an interesting way?	X		L: I could see and hear sights and sounds of the wetlands.
Does the book have an attractive cover?	X		S: *I worked hard on it.* L: It attracts attention. Makes me want to read it.
Does the title page have the book's title, the names of the author and publisher, and the place of publication?	X		L: I like your title.
Are there four or more pages with text and pictures about the wetlands?	X		S: *I have eight pages.*
Is there a list of the resources used to find the information?	X		L: Good variety of resources.
Is there a part that tells something about the author?	X		S: *I wrote about seeing Canadian geese on a fishing trip with my Dad.*

wealth of information about how students think, learn, and feel. They help us understand a student's internal thought processes. Rather than attempt to rate or score them for assessment purposes, however, it would be more meaningful to have students and their instructors select the log entries that reflect new insights and discoveries for inclusion in the process folios. Figure 9.10 is a student's journal response from the Wetlands unit. In this particular response, she explains how she came up with her research questions.

When she selected this particular log for her portfolio, the student explained the reasons for her choice as follows:

I picked this log because it shows how I came up with my questions. I started out asking why beavers build dams and why they don't get along with people. But when I did the web, I got a lot more ideas for questions to help me write my book. The most important questions were still about building dams and getting along with people.

Figure 9.10
Example of student log for the Wetlands unit

My topic is the beaver. I found out on the Internet that beavers change the land almost as much as men do. I was curious so I clicked on the beaver picture and found out that when they build dams, they make ponds and lakes. It also said that sometimes people and beavers don't get along. Now I had a lot of questions about beavers. The teacher said to make a web so I made one like we did in second grade. My main questions are in ovals. The rectangles show what I want to find out.

My Questions About Beavers

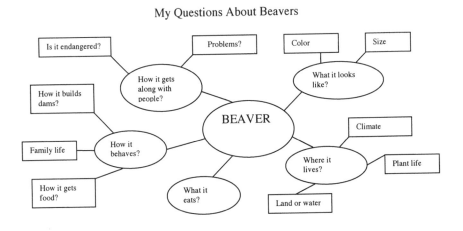

Step 6: Prepare a Summary Sheet for the Process Folio

The summary sheet helps make sense of the data contained in the process folio. As the first page of the document, the sheet provides a "big picture" view of what the student did, how his learning was measured, and the student's rating of his accomplishments. The actual work samples, assessment tools, student reflections, and instructors' comments come after the summary sheet as artifacts to document the learning achievements of a particular student.

Figure 9.11 is an example of a student's summary sheet for her Wetlands project. You will note that the teacher and library media specialist reviewed the student's comments and added their own. An agreement was reached with the student before assigning an overall rating representing the child's performance in relation to the specific standards addressed. The summary sheet displays the content standards addressed by the teacher as well as the information literacy standards addressed by the library media specialist.

Figure 9.11
Example of student's summary sheet for the Wetlands unit

Standards/Performance Indicators	What I Did (work samples)	How It Was Measured (assessment tool)	How Well I Did (rating)
Information Literacy			
Accesses information efficiently and effectively (AASL and AECT 1998) • Formulates questions based on information needs • Identifies a variety of information sources • Uses successful strategies for locating information	*I wrote five questions about my topic.* *I used books, encyclopedias, and the Internet.* *I wrote my search strategy in my journal.*	*I used the criteria for generating questions.* *I wrote everything on a resource matrix.* *My search strategy tells where I would look and words I would use.*	*My questions* <u>*meet*</u> *the standards.* *My matrix shows I* <u>*exceed*</u> *the standards.* *My search strategy* <u>*meets*</u> *the standards.*
Strives for excellence in information seeking and knowledge generation (AASL and AECT 1998) • Assesses quality of process and products • Devises strategies for revising, improving, and updating self-generated knowledge	*We made a list of criteria for our books.* *I went to lots of sources to get information and to check my facts.*	*I used the checklist to assess my work.* *I wrote in my journal about how I improved my work.*	*I* <u>*meet*</u> *the standards because I always assess my work.* *I* <u>*meet*</u> *the standards because I revise as I go.*
Science			
Develops understanding of • Characteristics of organisms • Life cycles of organisms • Organisms and environments (National Research Council n.d., online)	*I described the alligator in my book, and I talked about its life cycle.*	*I made sure that my information was accurate and important and that it answered the questions.*	*I* <u>*meet*</u> *this standard because I wrote about the alligator.*
Language Arts			
Conducts research on issues and	*I picked the*	*I used the chart that*	*I* <u>*meet*</u>

(Continued)

Figure 9.11 (*Continued*)

interests by generating ideas and questions and by posing problems (Kendall and Marzano 2004, online)	*alligator as a topic. I asked what it looks like, how it grows, and why it's in trouble.*	*says what makes a good question.*	*this standard because I asked good questions.*

Instructors' comments: We agree that your work meets the targeted standards for information literacy and language arts. However, more information is needed to answer all your questions. In particular, you need to explain the relationship between the alligator and the wetlands environment. We will discuss whether your work meets the standard for science.

Overall ratings:

Information literacy: Accesses information	Meets standard
Information literacy: Seeks information and generates knowledge	Meets standard
Language arts: Conducts research on interests and issues	Meets standard
Science: Understands organisms and their environments	Approaches standard

GETTING STARTED

Participating in portfolio assessment can be a daunting task. What must you consider? Where might you begin? First, teachers at your school must already be experimenting with portfolios. Second, you must be engaged in some level of collaborative instructional planning with your teachers. Third, you might consider the following strategy in experimenting with a portfolio system:

- Start with one teacher with whom you have successfully collaborated
- Together identify just one unit of work for the portfolio system
- Select no more than one or two information literacy standards as the targets for assessment in this unit (the teacher should also limit the content standards being addressed)

By limiting the number of teachers and students you are working with and by restricting the units and standards that you wish to assess, you make your initial work with portfolios more manageable. You also have an opportunity to test effective and efficient methods of data collection and organization.

CONCLUSION

With the current emphasis on performance assessment, an increasing number of schools have adopted a portfolio system to measure students' progress in relation to the standards. Donald Graves, however, states, "portfolios are simply too good an idea to be limited to an evaluation instrument" (1992, 1). He views portfolios as a way of helping students assume ownership of their own learning. By identifying work samples, assessing the quality of their performances, and reflecting on their successes and failures, students become the keepers of their portfolios. Students use them as a means of communication and self-discovery as well as assessment and evaluation.

If a school is already engaged in portfolio development, this presents a window of opportunity for an enterprising library media specialist to integrate evidence of students' learning achievements through the library media center. While portfolio assessment may be considered on the leading edge for many library media programs, developing this type of assessment information would make the benefits of learning through the library tangible and compelling.

REFERENCES

American Association of School Librarians, and Association for Educational Communications and Technology. 1998. *Information Power: Building Partnerships for Learning*. Chicago, Ill.: American Library Association.

Barrett, Helen C. 1997. "Collaborative Planning for Electronic Portfolios: Asking Strategic Questions." URL: http://transition.Alaska.edu/www/portfolios/planning.html (accessed Aug. 4, 2004).

Graves, Donald. 1992. "Portfolios: Keep a Good Idea Growing." In *Portfolio Portraits*, ed. Donald Graves and Bonnie Sunstein. Portsmouth, N.H.: Heinemann, pp. 1–12.

Kendall, John S., and Robert J. Marzano. 2004. *Content Knowledge: A Compendium of Standards and Benchmarks for K-12 Education*. 4th edition. Aurora, Colo.: Mid-Continent Research for Education and Learning. URL: http://www.mcrel.org/compendium/skillsIntro.asp (accessed July 8, 2004).

Kuhlthau, Carol. 1993. "Implementing a Process Approach to Information Skills: A Study Identifying Indicators of Success in Library Media Programs," *School Library Media Quarterly* 22, no. 1 (Fall): 11–18. URL: http://www.neutralbay-p.schools.nsw.edu.au/library/Kuhlthau.htm (accessed July 27, 2004).

Mundell, Susan, and Karen DeLario. 1994. *Practical Portfolios: Reading, Writing, Math, and Life Skills, Grades 3-6*. Englewood, Colo.: Libraries Unlimited.

National Research Council. n.d. *National Science Education Standards*. URL: http://www.nap.edu/readingroom/books/uses/html/ (accessed July 7, 2004).

Stiggins, Richard. 1997. *Student-Centered Classroom Assessment*. Columbus, Ohio: Prentice Hall, Inc.

Tuttle, Harry G. 1997. "The Multimedia Report: Electronic Portfolios Tell a Personal Story," *MultiMedia Schools* 4, no. 1 (January/February): 32–37. URL: http://www.infotoday.com/MMSchools/jan97/mms/portfol.htm (accessed July 24, 2004).

ADDITIONAL READINGS ON E-PORTFOLIOS

Ash, Linda E. 2000. *Electronic Student Portfolios, K-College*. Syracuse, NY: ERIC Clearinghouse on Information Resources. ED 448 285.

Farmer, Lesley S. J. 1997. "Tools for Electronic Portfolios," *Technology Connection* 4, no. 7 (December): 30–32, 47.

Garthwait, Abigail, and Jim Verrill. 2003. "E-Portfolios: Documenting Student Progress," *Science and Children* 49, no. 8 (May): 22–27.

Martin, Graham P., and Carter Burnette. 2000. "Maximizing Multiple Intelligences through Multimedia: A Real Application of Gardner's Theories," *MultiMedia Schools* 7, no. 5 (October): 28–30, 32–33.

McNulty, Kevin Y. 2002. "Fostering the Student-Centered Classroom Online," *T.H.E. Journal* 29, no. 7 (February): 16, 18, 20–22.

Penta, Mary Q. 2002. "Student Portfolios in a Standardized World," *Kappa Delta Pi Record* 38, no. 2 (Winter): 77–81.

Siegel, Del. 2002. "Creating a Living Portfolio: Documenting Student Growth with Electronic Portfolios," *Gifted Child Today Magazine* 25, no. 3 (Summer): 60–65.

Young, Jeffrey R. 2002. "E-Portfolios Could Give Students a New Sense of Their Accomplishments," *Chronicle of Higher Education* 48, no. 26 (March): A31–A32.

CHAPTER 10

Communicating Evidence of Learning

This chapter:

- Focuses on how assessment data collected in the library can be used to support school goals
- Makes a case for the importance of communicating assessment results to various stakeholders
- Provides scenarios and samples of how results can be synthesized and communicated to different audiences

The most critical uses of assessment data are to allow students an opportunity to reflect on their own progress and to provide instructors with crucial information on what students are learning and how teaching might be shaped to help students do even better. With the current emphasis on accountability, however, still another important use of assessment information has emerged: the need for synthesizing and presenting summaries of students' learning achievements to various stakeholder groups. In short, communicating evidence of what is being learned through library instruction is a valuable advocacy tool.

In this chapter, we share examples of how assessment data collected in the library can be shared with different school audiences. In the past, the evaluation of library media programs has been based on factors like circulation statistics, the size of the collection, the frequency of instructional sessions, and a physical count of students in the library. With the current emphasis on accountability and outcome-based instruction, the focus for evaluation has shifted from statistics about resources to the contributions made by the library media program to academic achievement. The critical question for twenty-first-century library media specialists is not "How many books are we circulating?" but "Are our programs and practices making a difference in terms of student learning?"

Ross Todd advises that key people, including teachers, administrators, and members of the larger community need to see "explicit local evidence of how collaborative learning communities can enable and foster significant learning outcomes of students" (2001, 1). As librarians work with teachers to plan a curriculum based on standards and grade level benchmarks, they

Figure 10.1
Steps involved in evidence-based assessment

Steps	Guiding Questions
1. **Collect** evidence of achievement.	What data do we collect to document learning?
2. **Analyze** evidence.	What does this data show?
3. **Synthesize** findings.	What conclusions can be drawn based on evidence?
4. **Communicate** results.	How do we report our findings?

need to systematically document the influence of information literacy instruction on the achievement of the school's learning goals.

HOW CAN ASSESSMENT DATA BE USED TO SUPPORT SCHOOL-WIDE GOALS?

In earlier chapters we described different assessment methods and the context in which they might be used to improve teaching and learning. In this chapter, we explore ways of using the same data to show how the library media program supports school-wide achievement goals. This involves taking assessment beyond its instructional applications and using it to validate the essential role of information literacy instruction in areas like critical thinking, problem solving, decision-making, and literacy.

Collecting evidence is not an end in itself. Todd (2001) stresses the importance of analyzing and synthesizing selected evidence to create an accurate picture of achievement. Figure 10.1 outlines a process that starts with data collection and ends with the communication of results.

WHY IS IT IMPORTANT TO COMMUNICATE RESULTS?

All instructors are being called upon to present evidence that their programs are contributing in a substantive way to student achievement. The question for library media specialists is: How can our assessment practices be used to show the link between information literacy instruction and student learning? We need to go beyond educated guesses and anecdotal reports by providing verifiable evidence that what we are doing does make a difference. From the plethora of data collected during the instructional process, evidence must be carefully selected for specific purposes, such as:

- Showing how libraries are helping students to meet the standards
- Confirming that students are learning to work as a group
- Validating the benefits of collaborative partnerships
- Demonstrating that students are able to locate, evaluate, and use information to construct knowledge of different disciplines

In the remainder of this chapter, we present several examples of how the assessment data might be summarized and communicated to different target audiences.

COMMUNICATING WITH TEACHERS

In one elementary school, the media center has always operated on a fixed schedule with half-hour sessions meeting every other week. In the past, the primary role of the library media specialist was to instruct students in the use of the library and to provide teachers with release time for planning. A new library media specialist has been hired. She wants to encourage more integrated and cooperative instruction. Three third-grade teachers accept her invitation to partner on a project. Together they develop and implement the Wetlands unit described in Chapter 6.

One of the instructional goals of the unit is for students to access and evaluate information found in both print and electronic resources. During planning meetings, teachers express some skepticism about how learning outcomes might be measured. They ask: "How do we know that this integrated approach to instruction will help our students meet grade level benchmarks?"

In the above scenario, the teachers have identified an information need. They want to see evidence that clearly shows how well their students are doing in terms of reading and understanding information found in various sources. With this as a starter, the library media specialist follows the steps laid out in Figure 10.1 to address the teachers' concerns.

Step 1: Collect Evidence of Achievement

The library media specialist decides that her first task is to show the correlation between the information literacy standard for accessing information and a related standard for reading—*Uses reading skills and strategies to understand and interpret a variety of informational texts.* (Although science standards are also addressed in the unit, teachers elect to assess science content using more traditional testing methods.) Her next step is to identify work samples, assessment tools, and reflections that document both language arts and information literacy standards. She collects the following pieces of evidence from each student:

- Responses to the journal prompt: "Which resources did you find most helpful? Explain why you think this."
- Resource matrix
- Rubric used to assess performance on the resource matrix

If you recall, a resource matrix (Figure 6.4) was used in Chapter 6 to guide students through the process of locating information about the Wetlands in a variety of sources. It is reproduced below (Figure 10.2). Completed matrices provided evidence of the students' ability to locate, evaluate, and compare information found in both print and electronic resources.

Figure 10.2
Matrix for identifying resources (work sample)

Link to the standards: In this lesson I will show that I can find information about my topic in different kinds of print and electronic resources.

RESOURCE MATRIX

The topic of my book is _____.

My research questions are

_____

_____

_____

The keywords I will use to search are _____.

Source of Information (Title)	Type of Information (Format)	One important thing I learned from the source

The most helpful resource I found was _____

The reason I think this is _____

Figure 10.3
Rubric for assessing the resource matrix (assessment tool)

Rating	Criteria
Does not meet standards	Does not include both print and electronic sources Takes notes from a single source Identifies only the resource that was used without explaining what was learned or how it was helpful
Approaches standards	Identifies both print and electronic sources Finds only one print and one electronic source Identifies what was learned from some resources Tells which resource was most helpful but doesn't explain why
Meets standards	Identifies both print and electronic sources Finds at least three different information sources Explains what was learned in each resource Tells which resource was most helpful and explains why
Exceeds standards	Identifies several print and electronic sources Uses four or more different information sources Explains what was learned in each resource Evaluates resources by explaining their strengths and weaknesses

The instructors use a rubric (Figure 10.3) to rate each student's resource matrix.

Step 2: Analyze Evidence

The real work of analysis is an ongoing and integral part of the instructional process. Students use the rubric as a guide as they work on their resource matrices. The same rubric provides a system for analyzing how well each student has achieved the desired outcome: to access and evaluate information in a variety of print and electronic sources. The resource matrix and the rubric, along with responses to the journal prompt, are analyzed to see what they say about each student's performance.

Step 3: Synthesize Findings

The library media specialist develops a profile that summarizes the data for a class. Figure 10.4 is a profile created for one of the three classes. Notice that comments are included to explain why some students exceeded or failed to meet standards.

A note about comments: Some teachers feel that a class profile is incomplete without some explanation about why a student received a particular rating. Teachers who feel this way may write comments for each student, or they may choose to comment only on performances at the

Figure 10.4
Sample of grade 3 class profile

Class List	Standards-based Assessment	Comments
Abigail	Exceeds	Identifies eight different sources and explains why some are better than others.
Benjamin	Meets	
Carrie	Meets	
Daniel	Approaches	
Emi	Exceeds	Finds five sources, both print and electronic. Tells something important learned from each. Identifies the best source.
Frank	Meets	
Isaac	Does not meet	Uses only one source—an encyclopedia. Does not evaluate or compare sources.
Jill	Approaches	
Kathryn	Meets	
Lily	Meets	
Mark	Meets	
Matthew	Exceeds	Identifies five sources of different kinds. Evaluates each source.
Nina	Meets	
Peter	Meets	
Ricky	Meets	
Sam	Approaches	
Suzie	Meets	
Tim	Exceeds	Identifies six sources, both print and electronic. Explains what was found in each.
Vanessa	Approaches	
Will	Meets	

extremes, those that do not meet or exceed the standards. Other teachers may write no comments at all. They believe that the ranking is all that is needed to synthesize the data. Since the comments do not factor into the final computation, they are an optional part of the class profile.

By creating profiles for all three classes, the instructors are able to compare and make the following types of generalizations:

• 5 percent of the students do not meet the standards.
• 20 percent of the students are approaching the standards.

- 55 percent of the students meet the standards.
- 20 percent of the students exceed the standards.

The library media specialist uses these conclusions to make the case that 75 percent of third-grade students involved in the project are either meeting or exceeding the criteria for accessing and evaluating information found in a variety of sources.

Step 4: Communicate Results

Communication can take many forms. In this case, the library media specialist shares the class profiles with the teachers in an informal setting that invites interaction and further analysis. The purpose of the meeting is to emphasize that the goals of information literacy and other content areas can be accomplished through a collaboratively planned, integrated unit of instruction. The results can now be used to plan future projects.

COMMUNICATING WITH PRINCIPALS AND SCHOOL COUNCILS

> Faced with budget cutbacks and limited resources, the principal of the middle school has asked the entire staff to submit evidence that their programs are contributing to the school's achievement goals. The school advisory council will use this information to make decisions regarding the allocation of personnel and fiscal resources for the coming school year.
>
> Recognizing the high stakes involved, the library media specialist seeks ways to correlate information literacy with the schoolwide goal to improve reading proficiency. Together with the eighth-grade teachers, she develops the literature-based unit described in Chapter 7. Students read a variety of literary genre and research different aspects of the Holocaust to answer the guiding questions: "Why is it important to remember the Holocaust?" and "How can we apply the lessons of the Holocaust to our lives today?" The library media specialist contributes to the unit by identifying appropriate literary selections and guiding students through the process of gathering information related to the Holocaust experience.
>
> In Chapter 7 we described two of the lessons conducted by the library media specialist:
>
> Lesson 1: Asking the right questions
> Lesson 2: Appreciating creative forms of expression

(Continued)

> Because the school's focus is on reading improvement, the library media specialist decides to use assessment data from the second lesson to show the relationship between information literacy instruction and the school-wide reading goal.

In the above scenario, the library media specialist seeks to answer the following questions:

- How does the library program contribute to the goal of improving reading comprehension?
- How can the contributions of information literacy instruction be validated?

Step 1: Collect Evidence of Achievement

The standards and performance indicators for reading and information literacy that have been identified for this unit (Figure 10.5) provide a starting point for the collection process.

Using the standards as a guide, the library media specialist collects evidence to show how information literacy instruction helps to bring about improvement in the area of reading. She selects the following documents:

- Literature response form
- Rubric for assessing the students' responses to literature

The Holocaust unit calls for students to select at least three titles from a list of Holocaust resources to read or view independently. The items they

Figure 10.5
Alignment of standards and performance indicators for reading and information literacy

Content Areas	Standards	Performance Indicators
Reading	The student reads a wide range of literature from many periods and in many genres to develop an understanding of the dimensions of human experience (NCTE/IRA 1995)	Uses reading skills and strategies to understand a variety of literary passages and texts (Kendall and Marzano 2004)
Information Literacy	The student who is an independent learner is information literate and appreciates literature and other creative expressions of information (AASL and AECT 1998)	Derives meaning from information presented creatively in a variety of formats (AASL and AECT 1998)

Figure 10.6
Literature response form

Link to standards: I will gain a deeper understanding of the Holocaust by reading and responding to a variety of literary pieces presented in different formats.

AUTHOR OR PERSON RESPONSIBLE: _____
TITLE: _____
FORMAT OR GENRE: _____

QUESTIONS	MY THOUGHTS	EVIDENCE FROM THE WORK
From whose point-of-view is the story told?		
How did the piece contribute to my understanding of the Holocaust?		
What did I like best or least about this piece?		
How does it compare to other things I have read or viewed about the Holocaust?		

choose must represent different genres and formats. For example, a student might choose to read a memoir and a play and to watch a video. The literature response forms (Figure 10.6) that he completes for each item are used to assess his proficiency in terms of the targeted standards.

The teachers, the library media specialist, and the students use a rubric (Figure 10.7) to determine how well students are responding to a variety of literary formats and genre.

Step 2: Analyze Evidence

The response form documents the student's ability to interpret a piece of literature in relation to the central theme and driving questions. The rubric is used to analyze how well students are able to read, interpret, and

Figure 10.7
Tool for assessing responses to literature

Rating	Criteria
Does not meet standards	Reading choices are limited to a single format or genre. A personal statement is included for only one or two of the four questions. There is no evidence from the work to support the statement(s).
Approaches standards	Reading choices are limited to a single format or genre. Personal statements are included for three of the four questions. There is limited evidence (one sentence) from the work to support each statement.
Meets standards	Reading choices represent three different formats and/or genres. Personal statements are included for all of the questions. There is satisfactory evidence (two or three sentences) from the work to support each statement.
Exceeds standards	Reading choices represent more than four formats and/or genres. Personal statements are included for all of the questions. There is strong evidence (more than three sentences) from the work to support each statement.

appreciate literature in different formats and genres. In this instance, the library media specialist wants to find out about the variety and range of the student's reading selections. She also examines the responses to determine how well students

- Identify the point of view expressed in the story
- Explain how the piece contributed to their understanding of the Holocaust
- Provide a personal perspective by stating what they liked best or least about the piece
- Compare pieces of literature on the Holocaust theme

Step 3: Synthesize Findings

The instructors use the rubric and share the task of analyzing each student's performance. The library media specialist records each student's rating on a class profile. At the request of the teacher, she also includes brief comments to justify each rating. One class's profile is displayed in Figure 10.8.

Figure 10.8
Sample of grade 8 class profile

Class List	Standards-based Assessment	Comments
Anita	Exceeds	Responds to five pieces of literature (a novel, two poems, a video, and a biography). Answers questions thoughtfully with reference to text.
Brian	Meets	Responds to a novel, a poem, and a video. Responses show insight into the tragedy of the event.
Cindy	Approaches	Reads only fiction pieces. Responses are very brief. No reference to text.
David	Exceeds	Completes response forms for four works (a video, a biography, a poem, and a history). Supports opinions with analysis of text/script.
Emily	Meets	Responds to a novel, a poem, and a TV show. Tells what she learned from each. Refers to text in her responses.
Frank	Meets	Responds to a TV documentary, a video, and a novel. Tells what he likes best about each and makes comparisons with books read in class.
Gina	Exceeds	Reads five pieces of literature (two novels, a biography, and two poems). Explains how each contributed to her understanding.
Heather	Approaches	Reading is limited to personal narratives. Says what she likes about each, but doesn't refer to text to answer most questions.
Ian	Meets	Responds to a novel, a video documentary, and a biography. Refers to text in his answers.
Jodi	Does not meet	Completes only one response form for a video. Responses are very general and lacking in detail.
Mike	Meets	Reads a novel and a biography. Also responds to a TV documentary. Makes good comparisons with specific references to text.
Patrick	Approaches	Reads two personal narratives. Tells what he thinks, but makes limited reference to text.

Data from the class profiles provide the following snapshot of students' achievement:

- 5 percent of students did not meet the standards.
- 15 percent of students are approaching the standards.
- 60 percent of students are meeting the standards.
- 20 percent of students exceed the standards.

Step 4: Communicate Results

The library media specialist decides that a multimedia slide presentation would be the most effective way to share her findings with the school advisory council. Her aim is to convince the council that information literacy instruction has a direct bearing on reading improvement. To make this correlation, she presents her evidence under the following major points:

- What she taught
- What students were expected to do (the performance task and the assessment criteria)
- How well students performed

The graph displayed in Figure 10.9 is used to make the point that 80 percent of the students either met or exceeded the targeted standards for reading and information literacy.

Figure 10.9
Profile of achievement

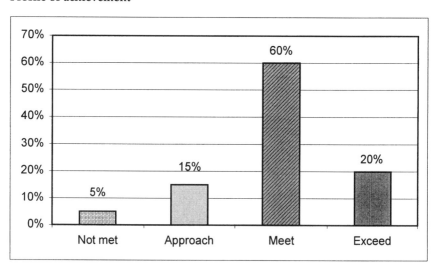

The library media specialist carefully words her presentation so that it is jargon-free, and it is warmly received. Lay members on the council are duly impressed and ask thoughtful questions about collaborative instruction and the involvement of the library media specialist. The presentation itself and the ensuing discussion provide convincing evidence that the library program has a significant role to play in achieving the school's goals. Accordingly, the council agrees to maintain the current funding for library resources and to seek cuts elsewhere in the school budget.

COMMUNICATING WITH THE LARGER COMMUNITY

There has been an ongoing debate within the community about whether students graduating from high school are adequately prepared to enter the workforce. A blue-ribbon panel, composed of community and business leaders, is set up to study the issue and make recommendations. The community group begins its investigation by identifying the skills and competencies needed in a twenty-first-century workplace. Among the skills they identify as most critical is the ability to use technology to perform workplace tasks.

During the fact-finding phase of the investigation, the panel asks the local high school to verify the place of educational technology in the curriculum. The school committee charged with providing this information organizes a presentation around four major themes:

- Technology as a tool for learning
- Technology as a tool for communication
- Technology as a tool for research
- Social and ethical issues related to the use of technology

In this scenario the community group wants to know what schools are doing to prepare students for a workplace driven by technology. The challenge for school personnel is to describe how technology-based activities help students to learn, to communicate, and to produce knowledge.

As a key member of the technology committee, the library media specialist agrees to address technology as a tool for research. He decides to focus his presentation on two phases of the search process where technology is used extensively: locating information and presenting knowledge.

Step 1: Collect Evidence of Achievement

For his part of the presentation the library media specialist randomly selects 30 (out of 200) senior projects representing a heterogeneous group of students and a diverse mix of topics and methodologies. Process folios

Figure 10.10
Sample of tally sheet

Student	Web Sites	Electronic Encyclopedia	Periodical Database	Video/TV	E-mail
Student 1					
Student 2					
Student 3					

for each of the selected projects are also assembled to document the research and production processes. The library media specialist plans to analyze and summarize information from the following items in the process folios:

- Annotated bibliographies prepared by students
- Plans for the final presentations
- Students' reflections on how they used technology to access information and make their presentations

The annotated bibliographies include citations for all of the resources used by students during the information search process. The library media specialist creates a tally sheet (Figure 10.10) to track the various types of technology sources cited by individual students in their bibliographies.

Early in the process, students begin working on their presentation plans. These plans are reviewed at different phases of the research. The library media specialist refers to the plans illustrated in Figure 10.11 to determine how many students used technology tools for their final presentations as well as the types of tools employed.

Step 2: Analyze Evidence

The library media specialist focuses on two questions related to the contributions of technology to the senior projects:

- How do students use technology to *locate* information?
- How do students use technology to *present* their projects?

To find out how technology is used to locate information, he gathers data by examining students' annotated bibliographies and making hash marks on the tally sheet (refer to Figure 10.10) to indicate sources that were accessed through technology.

Figure 10.11
Plan for presentation

The topic of my project: _____

My audience: _____

Date, time, and place of the presentation: _____

My statement of purpose (what I hope to show, do, or demonstrate): _____

How I will present my project: _____

Technology tools I plan to use:

____Video

____Presentation software (e.g., PowerPoint)

____Multimedia software (e.g., HyperStudio)

____Web authoring tool (e.g.,Web Site Word)

Other resources I will need: _____

Adjustments I made to my plan: _____

_____

His next step is to find out how many students use technology in their presentations. He gathers this information by examining students' presentation plans where they indicated the technology tools they planned to use and the adjustments they made to their plans. It is important to point out that although students are encouraged to incorporate multimedia, video, and Web technology into their presentations, the use of technology is not a requirement; nor is it always appropriate.

Finally, the library media specialist reviews students' reflections to find out how they felt about the contributions of technology to their projects. Students have been asked to reflect on these questions: What technologies did you use for your project? How did they contribute to the final outcome? Could you have done it without the technology? Here is how one student responds:

My project was about finding ways to protect our beaches from erosion. Most of my information came from the Internet. I found five different web sites on beach erosion that answered my research questions and that I could understand. I listed them in my bibliography. I also used e-mail to get information from an expert on beach erosion at the university. My bibliography also has his name and the dates when we corresponded.

I made a display board to show the results of my research, but I needed to use computers to show my data and to write my conclusions. I used a word processing program (Microsoft Word) and a graphics program for my graphs and charts. I could have drawn my figures, but it wouldn't have looked as good.

I don't think I could have done this project without technology. There aren't many books about beach erosion, and the information is outdated. The information on the Web is the most up-to-date. I also got a lot of help from the university professor. He is working on beach erosion in Hawaii and had a lot of data. He had one of his students answer the questions that I sent through e-mail. That was very helpful.

After reading the student's response, the library media specialist indicates with a plus sign that the student expresses a positive attitude toward technology use. He analyzes each student's response in the same way, using a minus sign for those who do not find it beneficial to use technology and an equal sign for those with a neutral attitude.

Step 3: Synthesize Findings

The library media specialist now has three sets of data to create a picture of how technology has been employed in the senior projects. Figure 10.12 shows the composition of these data sets.

Figure 10.12
Synthesizing data about the use of technology

	Purpose	Data Source	Data Collected
Set 1	Find out how students use technology to locate information	Annotated bibliographies Tool for analyzing bibliographies	Number of citations for technology-based resources Technology tools used to locate information
Set 2	Find out how students use technology to present knowledge	Plan for final presentation	Number of students who use technology to present Kinds of technology used to present
Set 3	Find out how students feel about technology use	Reflection logs	Attitudes toward technology use

Figure 10.13
Synthesizing data related to technology use

Technology Used to Locate Information (N=30)					
Web Sites	E-mail	Periodical Database	Electronic Encyclopedia	Video/TV	Total # of students using technology
///// ///// ///// ///// ///// /	////	///// ///// //	///// //	///// ////	///// ///// ///// ///// ///// /////
(26)	(4)	(12)	(7)	(9)	(30)
87%	13%	40%	23%	30%	100%

Technology Used to Present Knowledge (N=30)						
Video Production	Multimedia	PowerPoint	Web Authoring	Spreadsheet	Graphic Software	Total # of students using technology
////	///// /	///// ///	///	/	///// ////	///// ///// ///// ///// /
(4)	(6)	(8)	(3)	(1)	(9)	(21)
13%	20%	26%	10%	3%	30%	70%

Attitudes About Technology (N=30)		
Positive	Negative	Neutral
///// ///// ///// ///// ///// /	/	///
(26)	(1)	(3)
87%	3%	10%

Using hash marks to keep a running tally, the library media specialist tabulates the data. Figure 10.13 displays how many students use each type of technology as well as the total number of students using some form of technology to locate information and to present their projects. The library media specialist also keeps a tally on the attitudes expressed by students in their reflection journals.

Used in conjunction with samples of student work, summary data like this can make a compelling case that the technology enhances learning by increasing access to information and providing tools for productivity.

Step 4: Communicate Results

The presentation to the blue-ribbon panel is a collaborative effort involving the technology coordinator, a science teacher, the library media specialist, and two students who talk about how technology helped them with their projects. The group carefully plans the presentation to show

Figure 10.14
Percentage of students using technology to locate information

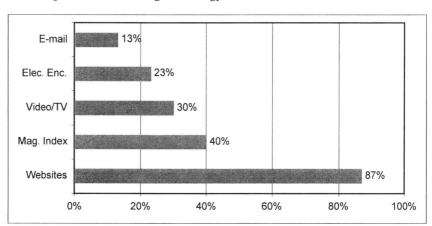

how technology-related activities in the school prepare students for a twenty-first-century workplace environment.

As mentioned earlier, the library media specialist is responsible for explaining how students used technology as a tool for research. He begins his portion of the group presentation by sharing several senior projects and engaging the audience in a lively discussion about how technology might have contributed to the outcome. Following the discussion, he shares a multimedia presentation emphasizing three important points:

- Point 1: Every student in our sample used at least one technology tool to locate information. The types of technology used are displayed in Figure 10.14.
- Point 2: In the sample of projects analyzed, 21 out of 30 students used some kind of technology in their presentations. Figure 10.15 shows the technologies used and the percentage of students who used each type of technology.
- Point 3: An analysis of students' journal entries shows that 26 out of 30 students believe that technology was a valuable tool for research. These attitudes toward technology are summarized in Figure 10.16.

The library media specialist uses the data to draw the following conclusions:

- With appropriate instruction, students become proficient at using technology to locate information.
- Given a choice, students use technology to make their presentations.
- Students who use technology in school develop positive attitudes toward technology as a tool for research and learning.

After the presentation, members of the blue-ribbon panel are encouraged to ask questions of the school representatives. The visual display of

Figure 10.15
Percentage of students using technology to present information

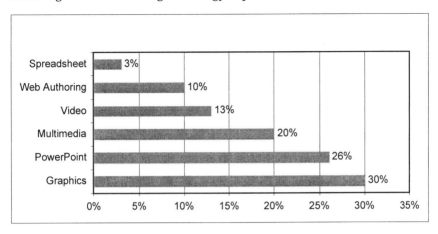

Figure 10.16
Student attitudes toward technology

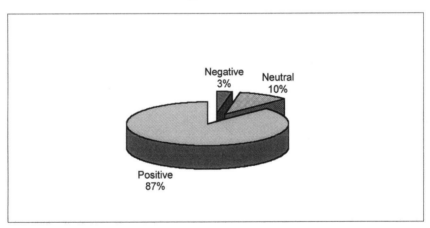

data, along with the work samples, assessment tools, and reflections woven into the presentation, help to convince the blue-ribbon panel that technology instruction has a critical role to play in developing technology-based research skills needed in the workplace.

CONCLUSION

At the most fundamental level, assessment provides both students and instructors with information about how well students understand and apply what they are learning. It also allows instructional partners to measure the effectiveness of their teaching and to use the information in shaping improvements. A third function of assessment is communicating the results to various stakeholders in the school community. This last chapter has focused on using assessment data in this way to "tell our story."

Evidence-based practice involves collecting critical assessment data but it does not stop there. It requires analyzing and synthesizing the information and being able to draw conclusions from it. Sharing these results with different stakeholder groups necessitates that the library media specialist

- Know what the stakeholder values and wants to know
- Identify the specific data that will answer the stakeholder's questions
- Assemble and present the evidence in a visually effective and verbally articulate manner

Providing tangible evidence about the power of learning through libraries is an enormous challenge facing our profession. It is a challenge we cannot afford to ignore if we are to be an integral part of the school's teaching and learning community. To be visible and influential partners in meeting the charge of schools—to prepare our students to be knowledgeable and responsible citizens—we must demonstrate and communicate how our instruction contributes to the school's learning targets. Assessing for learning cannot be an afterthought but must be a central part of our mission.

REFERENCES

American Association of School Librarians, and Association for Educational Communications and Technology. 1998. *Information Power: Building Partnerships for Learning.* Chicago, Ill.: American Library Association.

Kendall, John S., and Robert J. Marzano. 2004. *Content Knowledge: A Compendium of Standards and Benchmarks for K-12 Education.* 4th edition. Aurora, Colo.: Mid-Continent Research for Education and Learning. URL: http://www.mcrel.org/compendium/skillsIntro.asp (accessed July 8, 2004).

National Council of Teachers of English, and International Reading Association. 1995. *Standards for the English Language Arts.* URL: http://www.readwrite think.org/standards/ (accessed July 6, 2004).

Todd, Ross. 2001. "Evidence Based Practice II: Getting into the Action," *SCAN* 20, no. 1 (February): 1–8. URL: http://www.schools.nsw.edu.au/school libraries/scan/researchfeature.htm (accessed August 24, 2004).

Index

Adkison, Stephen, 3
Advisory councils: communicating
    with, 131–37
American Association of School
    Librarians (AASL), 5, 11, 13, 21,
    36, 111
Andrade, Heidi G., 22, 23
Aschbacker, Pamela R., 19, 27
Asp, Elliott, 6
Assessment: benefits to library media
    specialists, 6; benefits to students, 5;
    benefits to teachers, 6; criteria and
    tools for elementary school example,
    70, 72–73, 76; criteria and tools for
    high school example, 95–96, 100,
    101, 102; criteria and tools for
    middle school example, 82, 83–84,
    87–88, 89; defined, 1; vs. evaluation,
    1; examination of student work
    method, 13, 14, 15; impact of No
    Child Left Behind Act, 3–4; library
    media center overview, 10–17;
    methods overview, 13, 14, 15;
    observation method, 13, 14, 15;
    personal communication method,
    13, 14, 15; relationship to information
    literacy standards, 15–16; role of
    students, 2–3; in schools today, 1–3;
    summarizing and communicating
    data, 126–43; uses for data,
    125–26
Assessment tools, 13–14; checklists as,
    19–21, 22, 76, 77; conferences as,
    31–35; graphic organizers as, 49–66;
    logs as, 35–44; ratings scales as,

27–28, 29, 95, 96; rubrics as, 25–27,
    83, 84, 101, 102, 129, 133, 134;
    student portfolios as, 107–8
Association for Educational
    Communications and
    Technology (AECT), 5, 11,
    13, 21, 36, 111
Ausubel, David, 49
Authentic learning, 10–11; example,
    10–11; and goals of standards-based
    teaching, 11; and information
    literacy, 11–12

Backward planning, 14–16, 17. See also
    Outcome-based planning
Barrett, Helen C., 107
"Beginning with the end in mind." See
    Outcome-based planning
Bellanca, James, 59

Callison, Daniel, 4, 21, 49, 50
Chappuis, Stephen, 2
Checklists, 19–20; as assessment tool,
    19–21, 22, 76, 77; defined, 19;
    example, 22; how to construct,
    20–21; in Wetlands example, 76, 77;
    when to use, 20
Class profiles: elementary school
    example, 129–31; middle school
    example, 134–36
Coatney, Sharon, 1, 3
Community groups: communicating
    with, 137–43
Compare/contrast matrices. See
    Matrices

Concept maps, 50; defined, 50; howler
    monkey example, 55; how to
    construct, 52, 53; rain forest example,
    52–55; using to assess for information
    literacy, 52–55; when to use, 50, 52
Conferences, 31–32; as assessment
    tool, 31–35; defined, 31; example,
    34–35; how to structure, 33; how to
    use, 33–35; when to use, 31–32
Content standards, relationship to
    information literacy, 13
Curriculum planning. See
    Outcome-based planning

Davies, Anne, 13, 44
DeLario, Karen, 108
Donham, Jean, 1, 19
Donnelly, Amy, 10
Doyle, Christina S., 11

Education Commission of the States, 3
Egelson, Paula, 93
Eisenberg, Michael B., 3
Ekhaml, Leticia, 49
Electronic portfolios, 106–7
Elementary school example: com-
    municating with teachers, 127–31;
    outcome-based planning, 68–80
Enchanted Learning.com, 54
E-portfolios, 106–7
Evaluation vs. assessment, 1
Examination of student work: as
    assessment method, 13, 14, 15. See
    also Checklists; Graphic organizers;
    Rubrics; Student portfolios

Falk, Beverly, 6
Farmer, Lesley, 3, 4
Fishbone maps, 51

Grade school example: communicating
    with teachers, 127–31; outcome-
    based planning, 69–80
Graphic organizers, 49–50; as assess-
    ment tool, 49–66; concept maps,
    50–55; defined, 49; K-W-L charts,
    59–63; matrices, 63–66; webs, 56–59
Guskey, Thomas R., 3

Harada, Violet H., 12, 15, 35
Haycock, Ken, 4
Herman, Joan L., 1, 19, 27
High school example: assessing
    technology preparedness of
    students, 137–43; communicating
    with larger community, 137–43;
    outcome-based planning, 92–104
Holocaust display example: communi-
    cating with principals and school
    councils, 131–37; outcome-based
    planning, 81–91

Idea webs. See Webs
Information literacy, 11–12; and
    authentic learning, 11–12; checklists
    as assessment tool, 21, 76, 77;
    defined, 11; helping students
    assess sources, 73–76; helping stu-
    dents evaluate web sites, 94–99;
    helping students identify sources,
    70–73; matching assessment
    methods with, 15; rating scales as
    assessment tool, 27–28, 95, 96;
    relationship to assessment, 15–16;
    relationship to content standards,
    13; rubrics as assessment tool,
    25–27, 83, 84, 101, 102, 129, 133, 134;
    standards and performance indica-
    tors for elementary school example,
    70, 71, 73, 75; standards and per-
    formance indicators for high school
    example, 94, 100; standards and
    performance indicators for middle
    school example, 82, 83, 86–87
Instructional design. See Outcome-
    based planning
Instructional procedures: elementary
    school example, 73–75, 76, 78–79;
    middle school example, 84–86, 88,
    90; senior project example, 96–99,
    101, 103–4
International Reading Association
    (IRA), 13

Kuhlthau, Carol, 13, 110
K-W-L charts, 59; defined, 59; how
    to construct, 60–61; in pet project

example, 61–63; templates, 60, 61; as
type of graphic organizer, 51; using
to assess for information literacy,
61–63

Learning, authentic. *See* Authentic
learning
Library media centers: assessment in,
10–17; impact on learning, 4–5; what
to assess, 10–13
Library media specialists: analyzing
evidence of achievement in
information literacy, 129, 133–34,
138–40; benefits of assessment, 6;
collecting evidence of achievement
in information literacy, 127–29,
132–33, 137–38; communicating
results of achievement in
information literacy, 131, 136–37,
141–43; communicating with
multiple target audiences, 126–43;
communicating with principals
and school councils, 131–37;
communicating with teachers,
127–31; communicating with the
larger community, 137–43; and
information literacy, 11–12;
overview of assessment role, 5–7;
role in elementary school example,
70–76, 77, 78–79; role in high school
example, 93–101, 102, 103–4; role in
middle school example, 82–88, 89,
90; shift from focus on resources to
focus on student learning, 5, 6;
synthesizing findings of achievement in information literacy, 129–31,
134–36, 140–41; use of student
portfolios, 110–22
Loertscher, David V., 4
Logs, 35; as assessment tool, 35–44;
defined, 35; examples, 37, 38–39, 42,
43; facilitating use, 38–39; how to use,
38–44; using to assess for information
literacy, 40–44; when to use, 36–37
Luongo-Orlando, Katherine, 14, 101

Martin, Patty, 93
Martin-Kniep, Giselle, 48

Marzano, Robert J., 10, 63
Matrices, 63; compare/contrast, 63–66;
defined, 63; examples, 65; how to
construct, 63–64; in Kids Voting Program example, 64–66; model, 64;
template, 64; as type of graphic
organizer, 51; using to assess for
information literacy, 64–66, 70, 72,
73, 128; in Wetlands example, 70, 72,
73, 128; when to use, 63
McTighe, Jay, 14, 69, 101
Middle school example: communicating
with principals and school councils,
131–37; outcome-based planning,
81–91
Mills, Heidi, 10
Mitchell, Ruth, 14
Mundell, Susan, 108

National Academy of Sciences, 13
National Council of Teachers of
English (NCTE), 13
National Council of Teachers of
Mathematics, 13
Neuman, Delia, 7, 11
Newmann, Fred M., 10
No Child Left Behind (NCLB) Act:
impact on assessment, 3–4
Novak, Joseph, 50

Observation: as assessment method,
13, 14, 15. *See also* Checklists; Rating
scales; Rubrics
Ogle, Donna, 59
O'Grady, Alice, 93
Outcome-based planning, 14–16,
17, 68–69; vs. conventional
planning, 68, 69; elementary
school example, 69–80; high
school example, 92–104;
Holocaust display example, 81–91;
middle school example, 81–91;
sample lessons, 70–76, 77, 78–79,
82–88, 89, 93–101, 102, 103–4;
senior project example, 92–104

Pappas, Marjorie, 49
Partnership for 21st Century Skills, 4

Perkins, David N., 14
Personal communication: as
    assessment method, 13, 14, 15
Personal correspondence, 44; as
    assessment tool, 44–47; defined, 44;
    how to construct, 44–46; how to use,
    46–47; templates, 45, 46; using to
    assess for information literacy,
    46–47; when to use, 44
Pinker, Steven, 2
Planning. *See* Outcome-based
    planning
Portfolios. *See* Student portfolios
Principals: communicating with,
    131–37
Problem solving models, 51
Process folios: assessing, 122;
    determining standards for, 111–12;
    developing assessment tools and
    strategies, 112–14, 115; identifying
    work samples, 114, 116, 117, 118;
    student reflection logs in, 116,
    119–20; summary sheets in, 120–22;
    what to include, 110–22

Rating scales, 27; as assessment tool,
    27–28, 29, 95, 96; defined, 27;
    example, 29; how to construct,
    27–28; in senior project example, 95,
    96; when to use, 27
Response sheets, 88, 89
Rubrics, 21–22; as assessment tool,
    21–27, 83, 84, 101, 102, 129, 133, 134;
    defined, 21; example, 26; in Holocaust
    display example, 83, 84, 133, 134;
    how to construct, 23–24; in senior
    project example, 101, 102; in
    Wetlands example, 129; when to
    use, 22–23

Sample lessons: Holocaust display
    project, 82–88, 89, 90; senior project,
    93–101, 102, 103–4; Wetlands project,
    70–76, 77, 78–79
School councils: communicating with,
    131–37
Senior project example: assessing
    technology preparedness of

students, 137–43; communicating
    with larger community, 137–43;
    outcome-based planning,
    92–104
Stakeholders, 125–26
Stiggins, Richard J., 2, 23, 31, 107, 108
Strickland, James, 10, 20, 21
Strickland, Kathleen, 10, 20, 21
Stripling, Barbara, 11
Student portfolios, 106; as assessment
    tool, 107–8; audiences for, 109;
    defined, 106; electronic, 106–7;
    vs. other assessment tools, 107–8;
    reasons to use, 108–9; use by library
    media specialists, 110–22. *See also*
    Process folios
Students: benefits of assessment,
    5–6; role in assessment, 2–3; tools
    for assessing their performance,
    13–14

Tallman, Julie I., 6
Tchudi, Stephen, 3
Teachers: benefits of assessment, 6;
    communicating with, 127–31;
    elementary school example, 69–80,
    127–31; high school example,
    92–104, 137–43; Holocaust display
    example, 81–91, 131–37; middle
    school example, 81–91, 131–37;
    senior project example, 92–104,
    137–43; Wetlands example, 69–80,
    127–31
Technology: assessing student
    preparedness, 137–43
Todd, Ross J., 4, 5, 7, 21, 125, 126
Tree maps, 51
Tuttle, Harry G., 107

Vandergrift, Kay E., 56

Wavell, Caroline, 4
Webs, 56; colonial fair example, 57–59;
    defined, 56; examples, 58; how to
    construct, 57; as type of graphic
    organizer, 51; using to assess for
    information literacy, 57–59; when to
    use, 56

Wetlands example: communicating with teachers, 127–31; outcome-based planning, 69–80
Whelan, Debra L., 4
Wiggins, Grant, 2, 14, 69, 101
Williams, Dorothy A., 4

Wilson, Kathleen, 50
Winters, Lynn, 19, 27
Wiske, Martha S., 14
Woolls, Blanche, 4

Yoshina, Joan M., 15

About the Authors

VIOLET H. HARADA is Professor of Library and Information Science at the University of Hawaii where she also coordinates the specialization for school library media preparation. In her 35-year career she has been a secondary English teacher, an elementary school library media specialist, a state level administrator, and a curriculum designer. In her current research and publications, she focuses on inquiry-based approaches to information seeking and use and on the dynamics of collaborative instruction. With Joan M. Yoshina, she is the co-author of *Learning Through Inquiry: Librarian-Teacher Partnerships*.

JOAN M. YOSHINA recently retired from the Hawaii Department of Education after 34 years as an elementary and high school teacher, a language arts specialist, and a library media specialist. She worked in both elementary and middle school libraries in Oahu. Joan has also published articles on the information search process and integrated instruction, guest lectured at the University of Hawaii, and presented her work at both state and national conferences.